T5-CVB-160

Managerial Accounting

Third Edition

Cecily A. Raiborn

Loyola University - New Orleans

Jesse T. Barfield

Loyola University - New Orleans

Michael R. Kinney

Texas A&M University

Prepared by
Michael R. Kinney

Texas A&M University

 South-Western College Publishing
an International Thomson Publishing company I(T)P®

Cincinnati • Albany • Boston • Detroit • Johannesburg • London • Madrid • Melbourne • Mexico City
New York • Pacific Grove • San Francisco • Scottsdale • Singapore • Tokyo • Toronto

Accounting Team Director: Richard K. Lindgren
Sponsoring Editor: Alex von Rosenberg
Developmental Editor: Leslie Kauffman
Production Editor: Deanna Quinn
Marketing Manager: Matt Filimonov
Manufacturing Coordinator: Gordon Woodside

ISBN: 0-538-88515-7

1 2 3 4 5 6 GP 3 2 1 0 9 8

Printed in the United States of America

I(T)P®
International Thomson Publishing
South-Western College Publishing is an ITP Company
The ITP trademark is used under license.

CONTENTS

CHAPTER 1
OPERATING IN A GLOBAL BUSINESS ENVIRONMENT

Questions

1. A mission statement is important to an organization because it provides a clearly worded view of what the organization wants to accomplish and how the organization uniquely meets its targeted customers' needs with products and services. Without a mission statement, an organization may veer away from its "view of itself" and find that it is engaging in activities that are not, nor ever can be, part of what it wants to do.

3. Goals are qualitative expressions of desired results. Objectives are quantifiable expressions of desired results. With respect to this course, your goal may be to demonstrate basic competency in the field of management accounting. Consistent with this goal, your objective may be to achieve a minimum grade of B.

5. Pure centralization is appropriate in very small firms that lack a pool of talented managers to make decisions. In this organizational setting, decisions are best made by experienced decision makers who possess the "vision" of the organization's future.

   Pure decentralization would be appropriate in an organization that has global operations that are very diverse in terms of their cultural and political settings. Pure decentralization is appropriate also in firms that face very competitive local markets that are sensitive to local information. Pure decentralization appropriately allows local managers to make most decisions because they are in the best position to have all information required to identify and evaluate the decision alternatives.

Chapter 1
Operating in a Global Business Environment

7. Many companies are relying more on outsourcing for certain inputs simply because the suppliers possess the knowledge and skills to more effectively do some tasks. For example, if a firm needs a world class information management system and lacks the internal abilities necessary to design such a system, that firm may rely on an outside consulting organization (such as Andersen Consulting) to design and implement such a system.

9. Human and structural capital are both elements of a firm's intellectual capital. Human capital reflects the knowledge and creativity of an organization's people, is the source of strategic innovation and renewal, and provides the foundation for core competencies. Structural capital consists of information systems, organizational structure, and "hard" organizational capabilities (items that can be owned and exchanged); structural capital allows human capital to be utilized.

    Students will have differing answers to the second part of this question, but some observations follow:

    o   In a start-up software development company: human capital is absolutely essential but, without structural capital, any software ideas could not be tested and debugged.

    o   In a car dealership: structural capital is probably more important because it would allow the dealership to determine where a specific automobile is, when it could be obtained, and how financing can be arranged. (Note: Cars can now be purchased from the Internet without any involvement of humans.)

    o   In a university: human capital may be more important. Consider that the University of Phoenix operates with little structural capital, but takes advantage of the skills of many, many humans in course design, development, and presentation.

    o   In a hospital: human capital may be more important because machines are not currently available that can do surgery or comfort patients. However, a hospital that lacks significant structural capital in today's world is probably not a place to which someone wants to go.

    o   At Coca-Cola: structural capital may be more important because of the need for product consistency throughout the world. Although new products are important, Coke's primary products (Coca-Cola Classic, Diet Coke, and Sprite) are possibly "world-class" enough to ensure the organization's longevity.

11. Workforce diversity may affect organizational culture because the work ethic of individual workers may be less homogeneous, communication may become more difficult, and observation of different religious holidays may create difficulties or new patterns of absenteeism. As diversity of the workforce increases, organizational culture must change to reflect the diversity.

    Some potential benefits of having workforce diversity include an opportunity to reduce prejudices, having workers who prefer different holiday schedules (minimizing the need for closure for specific holidays), and having workers who have different workplace characteristics (for example, some cultures may prefer to work in groups, others alone).

    Some potential difficulties of having workforce diversity include the possibility of different work ethics (for example, some cultures may perform at different "speeds," desire different workplace "formats" such as an afternoon siesta, or view communication within the workplace about outside activities differently). There may also be less tolerance if one employee group demands a greater number of religious holidays than another or a lack of understanding of why a particular employee (or employee group) does not believe in the need for a specific holiday that the majority observe.

13. In pure competition, there are many firms (such as supermarkets) which each have identical products and with no firm dominating. In monopolistic competition, there are many firms (such as shoe manufacturers), each with some product differentiation. In a monopoly, there is one seller with total control of price (such as the local water company). In an oligopoly, there are few firms (such as Internet providers--although there are about 4,000, a handful of companies split about 90% of the market), each with either differentiated or standardized products.

15.   A company may choose to avoid competition through
      compression of competitive scope (focusing on a specific
      market segment to the exclusion of others), differentiation
      (adding enough value to charge a higher price), and cost
      leadership (becoming the low-cost producer and, thus, low-
      price seller).
           The benefits of compressing scope allows for a
      limitation of advertising and a more complete understanding
      of the organization's customers. The latter lets the
      organization focus on delivering new products that are
      designed to appeal to the specific customer base.
           Differentiation is beneficial because the additional
      value allows the firm to charge a higher price and,
      hopefully, make a greater return than nondifferentiated
      companies.
           Cost leadership is beneficial because, at least until
      competitors benchmark the organization to learn its cost
      "secrets," the organization should be able to increase
      volume and generate higher profits. These organizations
      commonly take full advantage of the economies of scale.

17.   The primary management functions are planning, controlling,
      evaluating performance, and decision making. Planning is the
      process of translating goals and objectives into the
      specific activities and resources required to achieve those
      goals and objectives. Controlling is the exerting of
      managerial influence on operations so that they will conform
      to plans. Performance evaluation is the process of
      determining the degree of success in accomplishing a task.
      Decision making is the process of choosing among the
      alternative solutions available for a particular course of
      action. Thus, the latter three functions all follow from the
      planning process: without plans, there can be no control;
      determination of success will be impossible; and the courses
      of action that are available become infinite because there
      is no specified direction.
           Students will all have different examples of
      information needs for the various functions.

19.   Key variables are those factors that are most important to
      the organization's ability to achieve its goals. There are
      internal key variables that are susceptible to managerial
      control (such as product quality and customer satisfaction)
      and external key variables that are beyond managerial
      control (such as foreign exchange rates and the political
      situation in countries of operations). Knowledge of key
      variables is essential to the planning process so that
      managers are acutely aware of what issues need to be
      addressed to fulfill the specified goals and objectives.

21. A primary role of information is to reduce the uncertainty that otherwise exists in making decisions. The more important a decision to be made, the more information needs to be gathered and analyzed. Consider, for example, many students' decision to attend college: catalogs of alternative colleges are obtained; campus visits are made; financial aid packages are compared; program requirements are analyzed, etc.

23. This statement is false. Even small companies now have opportunities to arrange partnering with companies in other countries. These opportunities have become available, in part, because of the reduction in tariffs among countries and because of the ability to travel and communicate easily among countries.

25. Achieving a single market in Europe hinges on the member countries' willingness to conform to the market's rules. This, in turn, requires member nations to relinquish some autonomy to a market-level government or, alternatively, to adjust their laws and trading regulations to a common standard. Given that existing differences in laws reflect differences in cultures, political ideologies, and religion, harmonization of all relevant laws will require difficult compromises for member countries. In Europe, the biggest obstacle to completely integrated markets is likely to be differences in member nations' political ideologies.

    Different students will have chosen different factors and offer different suggestions for overcoming those obstacles.

27. In general, government regulations exist to protect the people and the environment, and to provide a climate for fair business competition. Typically, regulations exist that prescribe practices with respect to labor, product safety, appropriate conduct in foreign business transactions, and fair trade. Students from different countries should be asked to compare their answers and perceptions.

29. There are many self-serving reasons to be a nonpolluter. For example, a proactive strategy to reduce pollution may attract environmentally conscious consumers. Further, such an approach may avoid subsequent regulation of operations by government and may avoid legal entanglements caused by retroactive application of new laws.

31. A code of ethics is essential in any organization so that each member of the organization understands his/her moral obligations to other members of the organization. A code of ethics will help frame organizational culture--if, in fact, it is believed in and abided by organizational members at all levels and if there are penalties for violations from the code that are enforced.

33. The three generic missions are build, hold, and harvest. The build mission is to acquire market share and establish a position for future profitability. The hold mission is to hold existing market share or existing profitability. The harvest mission is to generate cash and profits for the organization which can be used to fund the growth areas of the firm.

    The generic mission and product life cycle may be highly correlated. For example, if divisions are established along product lines, each division's mission can be defined in terms of the mission of the product line. Accordingly, the product lines that represent the future of the company are likely to be assigned to divisions with a build mission. Similarly, product lines that represent a large portion of current profits and cash inflows are likely to be assigned to divisions that are charged with a hold or harvest mission.

35. The statement is false. Today, many companies have virtually no control over prices. Rather, prices are determined by impersonal market forces. Profitability is achieved by providing products at the market price and managing costs such that the market price exceeds the sum of all costs. Only if a company can somehow differentiate its products from its competitors can it attain some control over price.

    Consider, for example, the situation of Internet access. In February 1998, AOL announced a $2 increase to its "all-you-can-surf" service fee (up from $19.95 to $21.95). Because AOL has about 60% of the U.S. residential subscriber market, the fee for all service providers was expected to increase. Part of the need to raise fees stemmed from a need to add network capabilities to compete in the flat-rate service market--which created a huge increase in AOL's customer base.

37. Managers must be able to effectively balance short-term and long-term considerations in today's business environment because each depends on the other to ensure organizational survival. If an organization does not have short-term profitability and continuously innovate to keep pace with market demands, it has no chance of long-term survival. Alternatively, an organization who plans for the long-term but ignores those activities that are necessary in the short-term will also have no chance of long-term survival.

Exercises

39.

a.	3	f.	5
b.	6	g.	10
c.	8	h.	9
d.	1	i.	4
e.	2	j.	7

41. Each student will have different answers. However, the following items may be mentioned.

    a. Employees might be empowered to decide how long it will take to clean the houses to which they are assigned, how their schedules will be arranged so that all assigned houses are cleaned on time, what activities need to be performed to make the house clean, what equipment and supplies are to be used in the cleaning process, and where (and what) supplies are to be purchased. Employees are in a much better position to judge these issues than an absentee owner. With the input of the employees (as well as approval by you), a standard definition of "clean" that all employees would agree on should be determined.

    b. As the owner, you may retain the billing and supply purchasing processes as well as marketing and customer service. You would also probably want to retain the determination of customer satisfaction through surveys or telephone calls. These matters will be essential to your business profitability and longevity and the employees that you have may not have the expertise or ability (in the form of equipment or knowledge) to engage in these matters.

43. a. The primary benefits of outsourcing the collection function would be to have this function performed by a person or company who could perform the task at a lower cost and more effectively than it could be performed in-house and to eliminate a non-core competency and be able to focus more on jewelry purchasing and sales.

    b. The primary risks of outsourcing the collection function would be that the person or company providing the service is unethical and misrepresents the amount of collections that have been obtained and that the person or company is less concerned about whether all reasonable collection activities have been utilized (because it's not "their" money).

45. Each student will have different answers. No solution is provided.

Chapter 1
Operating in a Global Business Environment

47. a.   The costs of translating and reviewing the translation would be the largest costs associated with the additional information. (The cost of the additional pages in the annual report would be nominal.)

        Callaway competes using a differentiation strategy: as stated on the inside cover of the annual report, "Callaway Golf Company, through the use of technology, designs and manufactures premium, innovative golf clubs that are demonstrably superior to, and pleasingly different from its competition. The Company's golf clubs are sold at premium prices to both average and skilled golfers on the basis of performance, ease of use and appearance." Given this strategy and the fact that 32 percent of the company's sales in 1996 were in non-U.S. markets, the benefits derived from such translations are probably substantial: it indicates to all readers the high degree of importance that the company places on its international focus and business opportunities. It also highlights the significance of the acquisition of a majority interest in the company's German distributor. An additional benefit might be that, by making the management letter more readable by foreign investors, there could be an increased investment interest.

     b.   Each student will have different answers, but may indicate a need for the company's mission statement, future international acquisition or diversification plans, product development and introduction plans, and utilization of international suppliers within the company's value chain.

49. a.   Each student will have different answers, but may include the following: strategic (competitors, diversity, reputation, enforcement of a standard code of ethics, etc.); operating (worker availability, worker training, physical plant protection, size of branch location, installation and quantity of technology such as ATMs, etc.); financial (loan management, availability of capital, fund reserve requirements, etc.); and information (reliability of video camera operations for branch and ATMs, accuracy of strategic assumptions, accuracy of recordkeeping, etc.)

     b.   Each student will have different answers depending on what items were selected for discussion. No solution provided.

Cases

51. a.   A mission statement adds strength to an organization's strategic planning process by providing a clear view of what the organization wants to accomplish and how it uniquely meets customers' needs with products and services. Without a mission statement, an organization may find that it is engaging in activities that are not, nor ever can be, part of what it wants to do or is most competent to do.

    b.   A mission statement should be developed using input from everyone in the organization. If handled in this manner, the statement will become internalized by the organization members and become a distinct part of organizational culture.

    c.   In developing a mission statement, organizational members need to consider the organization's strengths and weaknesses (including core competencies), opportunities for growth, customer base (current and desired), competition, constraints (whether physical, financial, technological, regulatory, etc.), profitability, and employees' skills (current and those that can be obtained through training).

    d.   Each student will have a different answer. No solution provided.

53. a.   Overseas customers may not have access to the information needed to call up Dell and order a computer. They might be less aware of what Dell has available to offer than customers in the United States who may be more sophisticated computer purchasers.

    b.   Each student will have a different answer. No solution provided.

    c.   Tactical planning must occur to assure that Dell's strategic plans are being sought after on a short-term basis. Because Dell works so closely with customers, tactical planning can be directly affected by their needs and wants.

55. Each student will have different answers. No solution provided.

57. a.   The following competitive influences may affect each of
          the business choices:
          Cable company: with passage of the Telecommunications
          Act, many providers are entering the cable market, thus
          creating an unknown marketplace
          Airline: other major airlines as well as regional
          competitor, whether to operate at "hubs," and landing
          fees charged at different airports
          Hot-sauce plant: access to suppliers and plant
          capacity, permits to build, access to qualified
          employee base
          Fast-food: political climate, access to suppliers,
          dilution of disposable income of populace, first-mover
          advantage

     b.   The following competitive tactics may relate to each of
          the business choices:
          Cable company: cost leadership, confrontation
          Airline: product/service differentiation, cost
          leadership
          Hot-sauce plant: cost leadership, compression of scope,
          product/service differentiation, confrontation
          Fast-food: confrontation, cost leadership,
          product/service differentiation

     c.   The most important key variables for each business
          might include:
          Cable company: customer service, number of channels
          offered
          Airline: customer service, flight frequency, size and
          features of planes
          Hot-sauce plant: quality, price, flavor
          Fast-food: price, quality, location

     d.   Each student will have different answers. No solution
          is provided.

59. a.   A strategic alliance would be considered illegal in the
          United States when it interfered with free trade--for
          instance, if price fixing occurred among organizations.

     b.   Each student will have different answers, but they may
          mention issues such as establishment of a consistent
          source of supply (both in quantity and quality), of a
          strong customer base, of integration of activity (such
          as airline, hotel, car rental alliances), and so forth.

     c.   Each student will have different answers. No solution
          is provided.

61. a. Each student will have different answers. No solution is provided.

    b. You should discuss the ideas of exposure to liability and criminal prosecution for fraud, basis for public and competitor criticism for deceitful advertising, and loss of public goodwill with the Vice President of Marketing. You could discuss the possibility of changing the advertising campaign to provide a basis for the increased costs--informing the public that the "best ingredients cost a little more." Then, if all else fails, you need to decide if this is the type of business for which you want to work.

63. Each student will have different answers. No solution is provided; however, it is essential that students realize that computer software piracy is an illegal as well as unethical activity (because it is theft).

65. a. The quote indicates that the predominant concern of American businesses should be the generation of profits. There is nothing explicit or implied in the statement to indicate the profits must be derived from that set of activities that is legal within the local jurisdiction. Given that the pursuit of profit is constrained to legal activities, Friedman's statement is merely a pro-capitalism statement.

    b. Ethically, one might feel that the pursuit of profit should be constrained such that profit is not pursued to the detriment of human life, human happiness, the environment, etc. In short, ethically, one might easily identify several objectives that managers should hold in preference to maximization of profit.

    c. If one takes a long-term view of a manager's job, it might be logical to argue that the profit-maximizing actions of managers are those actions that are both legal and ethical. That is: unethical and illegal actions, in the long term, are not optimal from the view of maximizing profit. Illegal actions draw fines, lawsuits, new regulations, and other costly sanctions in the long term. Unethical acts in the long term create loss of business reputation, loss of customers, and loss of market share. Hence, in the long run, there may be no conflict between Friedman's statement as to managers' obligations and the legal and ethical obligations of managers.

67. a. Andrea Nolan's ethical responsibilities require that she not tell her friend, Ron Borman, about EraTech's cash flow problems. In accordance with Statement on Management Accounting Number 1C (SMA 1C), Andrea Nolan, as a management accountant, must comply with the following standards for ethical conduct:
    o **Confidentiality.** Nolan must refrain from disclosing confidential information acquired in the course of her work except when authorized, unless legally obligated to do so. In this situation, Nolan is neither authorized nor has a legal obligation to do so.
    o **Integrity.** Under this standard for ethical conduct, Nolan has the responsibility to:
    --refrain from engaging in any activity that would prejudice her ability to carry out her duties ethically.
    --refrain from either actively or passively subverting the attainment of the organization's legitimate and ethical objectives.

    b. Andrea Nolan has an ethical responsibility to inform EraTech that Ron Borman has decided to postpone the paper order. As a management accountant, Nolan must comply with the following standards of ethical conduct as prescribed by SMA 1C:
    o **Confidentiality.** Nolan should refrain from appearing to use confidential information acquired in the course of her work for unethical advantage, either personally or through third parties.
    o **Integrity.** Under this standard for ethical conduct, Nolan has the responsibility to:
    --refrain from either actively or passively subverting the attainment of the organization's legitimate and ethical objectives.
    --communicate unfavorable, as well as favorable, information and professional judgments or opinions.

    c. In accordance with SMA 1C, Andrea Nolan should resolve this matter by discussing the situation with her immediate superior. Nolan should tell her superior of her longtime friendship with Ron Borman; however, she should make it clear that she has not and will not disclose confidential company information to Ron Borman or any other outside party except when authorized or legally obligated to do so. If a satisfactory resolution to the problem is not achieved, Nolan should submit the matter to the next higher managerial level; however, she should inform her immediate superior that she is going to take this step.

(CMA)

CHAPTER 2
INTRODUCTION TO COST MANAGEMENT SYSTEMS

Questions

1. All control systems rely on information. Information is needed regarding expected performance and actual performance. An effective control system requires both types of information.

3. The four components are a detector, an assessor, an effector, and a communications network. These components can be related to the climate control system in an automobile. The driver sets the climate control at a desired temperature. A detector measures the actual temperature in the car; the assessor compares the desired temperature to the actual temperature; the effector causes either heated or cooled air to be released into the car. The communications network allows information to be conveyed between the detector and the assessor and then between the assessor and effector.

5. Costs could be minimized by simply having no operations, no investment, and no other organizational activities. Hence, costs are a necessary obstacle to generation of revenues. Thus, the objective is not to minimize costs but to maximize the benefits that are derived from cost incurrence.

7. *Financial accounting:* information about valuation of inventories, other assets, and cost of goods sold.
Production reporting: measurement of product cost and production volume, cost of labor, cost of overhead and materials consumed.
Inventory management: cost of carrying inventory, cost of making inventory, cost of inventory outages.
Production planning and scheduling: historical information regarding product demand, projections on future product demand, setup costs, inventory storage costs, economic order quantity.
Research and development: estimation of R&D cost, estimation of expected benefits from R&D activities, product life cycle information, tax benefits of R&D.
Quality control: cost of quality assessment, cost of quality failure (internal and external), rate of quality defects, various measurements of achieved quality.
Marketing: costs of alternative product promotion strategies; information regarding product distribution costs; product sales information by area, product, salesperson; life cycle product costs, profitability measurements.

9. *Research and development:* GAAP-based rules require these costs to be expensed as incurred. For internal purposes, however, managers may want to match these costs with the benefits they generate: new products and services.
   Subunit costs: For internal purposes, costs may be tracked to individual subunits so that the contribution of subunits to corporate profits may be assessed. For external purposes, costs will likely be reported only for the entire entity.
   Life-cycle considerations: For internal reporting purposes, costs may be maintained on a life-cycle basis to better associate cause and effect; for external reporting, the firm will likely use period-by-period reporting to be in compliance with GAAP.

11. Product costs are costs that are incurred in connection with the production of a product or service. Period costs are all other costs. The distinction is important for managing costs because the management of costs depends on identifying the activities that cause costs to be incurred. Product costs are caused by production activities; period costs are caused by other activities.
    The distinction is also important for financial accounting purposes as generally accepted accounting principles require product costs to be reported separately from period costs.

13. The major distinguishing factor between manufacturing and merchandising firms is the degree of conversion that occurs within each type of firm. Manufacturing firms are characterized by a high degree of conversion; merchandising firms are characterized by a low degree of conversion.

15. Normal costing allows firms to make more timely decisions because it is a system that is partly based on estimated rather than actual costs. Because actual costs are not known for some cost items until the end of the accounting period, an actual cost system cannot provide timely information **during** a period.
    However, if estimates of the actual costs are used, the estimates can be made prior to the start of a period and timely information can be provided by the costing system as the period progresses. The necessity of waiting until the period ends to determine costs is avoided.

17. Organizational culture can be an effective control device. A culture is a reflection of the values and practices that are acceptable or preferred by the company. The mere existence of the culture deters certain undesirable practices and encourages others. The culture can be perpetuated by hiring people who have values that are consistent with the culture. In this manner, the culture is perpetuated and the employees have homogeneous beliefs regarding the culture.

Organizational culture can also affect a firm's ability to manage costs because it affects attitudes and actions of employees. For example, if the culture is one that empowers employees and makes employees responsible for outcomes, employees will actively seek opportunities to reduce costs. In this instance, the culture will be an effective cost management tool. However, if the culture is one that provides little incentive and little opportunity for employees to participate in cost reduction, then the culture will impede the organization's ability to effectively manage costs.

19. A high level of variable costs and a low level of fixed costs is ideal in a down-trending economy. As the deteriorating economy causes sales to fall, costs fall almost proportionately. At the extreme, a company with only variable costs could have sales fall to $0 without incurring a loss. The benefits of having a cost structure that is mostly fixed are realized in an up-trending economy. As sales rise, costs remain nearly constant; the result is that profits rise by nearly the same amount as sales.

21. The cost management systems of a firm with a high level of fixed costs would need to concentrate on the events that give rise to fixed costs, e.g., making new investments. Since many fixed costs are not controllable once the investment has been made, much of the cost control management would be focused on investing activities. A firm with mostly variable costs would concentrate its cost management on controlling volume and controlling the prices, quality and unit quantities of volume-based inputs.

23. Feeder systems are the individual systems that provide the information to the cost management system (e.g., payroll system, accounts payable, accounts receivable). These systems are very important to the design of a CMS because they determine the type, format, and amount of information gathered. One primary consideration is to be certain that there is compatibility among the many feeder systems. Additionally, when gap analysis is conducted, any additional information that is needed may be acquired from an existing feeder system.

25. They are equally important. They are all integral to the design of an effective cost management system. Only if all three elements are designed properly will the cost management system serve to effectively and efficiently implement the firm's strategies.

27. Students should have little difficulty thinking of incidents where the relationship between behaviors and performance evaluation is evident. Sometimes the behavior exhibited is positive and sometimes it is negative. For example, by grading based on class participation, a professor may get students to be more involved in class discussions. By giving certain types of exams, a professor may encourage students to memorize facts. By providing demerits for missing class, a professor may encourage high class attendance. By rewarding only research productivity, a university may encourage professors to be uncaring about the quality of their teaching.

29. Gap analysis is the formal comparison of the ideal cost management system of a specific firm to its existing cost management system.

    Gap analysis is used to update cost management systems by bringing focus to the differences between the existing system and an ideal system. These differences or "gaps" are the areas in which managers strive to make improvements.

Exercises

31. a. F
    b. F
    c. M
    d. M
    e. F
    f. M
    g. F
    h. M
    i. M
    j. F
    k. M
    l. F
    m. M
    n. M

33. a. M MD S
    b. M (possibly S)
    c. M MD
    d. M MD
    e. M MD S
    f. M S
    g. M MD (possibly S)
    h. MD
    i. S
    j. M MD S
    k. M
    l. M MD S

35. a.   PD
     b.   PR
     c.   PR
     d.   PD
     e.   PD
     f.   PR
     g.   PR
     h.   PD
     i.   PD
     j.   PR
     k.   PD
     l.   PD

37. Students should discover that this ratio will vary widely
     across industries. For example, grocers operate on very thin
     gross margins; such firms should have a very high ratio of cost
     of goods sold to sales. In general, this will be true of many
     industries that have a relatively low degree of conversion.
          In other industries, the costs of distribution and
     marketing consume a relatively large portion of sales. These
     industries will be characterized by a low ratio of cost of
     goods sold to sales.

39. The oral report should stress that in the growth-oriented
     firm, much of the accountant's time would be dedicated to
     issues encountered in the growth strategy; for example:
     acquisition of capital for expansion, managing the target cost
     of new products, developing and instituting control systems to
     implement the growth strategy, and developing life-cycle cost
     estimates.
          Similarly, the report should stress that in the mature
     firm, the focus would be on generation of profits and cash
     flow. Accordingly, much time would be dedicated to developing
     and managing operating budgets, cash flow information, and
     control systems that focused on cash and profit generation.
     Additionally, the accountant would provide information to
     managers to support decisions about when to abandon or dispose
     of unprofitable products that have reached late stages of their
     life cycles.

Cases

41. a.   Agco has developed a strategy of competing on price. The
          firm is not an innovator, nor does the firm have a
          technological advantage over its competitors. The firm's
          main critical success factor is to respond quickly to the
          innovations of its competitors by duplicating their new
          products and selling them at a lower price.

               Deere & Co. competes on the basis of producing
          products of a very high quality with innovative features.
          The firm must maintain a strong research and development
          effort to support quality improvements and develop new
          products.

     b.   Some of the most significant components of Agco's cost
          management system would be
          · systems to monitor new product offerings of
            competitors;
          · systems to design new products based on the technology
            used by competitors;
          · target costing system to manage the cost of acquiring
            components in new products;
          · systems to manage the quality and quantities of
            purchased components--this would include systems to
            screen potential suppliers;
          · systems to tear down and reverse engineer competitors'
            products;
          · cost control systems to keep downward pressure on costs
            throughout the product life cycle--a low price strategy
            depends critically on the ability to produce products
            at costs below those of competitors;
          · systems to gather industry level intelligence data that
            help managers determine what future sales volumes are
            likely to be for various potential products.

          Some of the most significant control systems at Deere &
          Co. would include
          · systems to manage product development; among these
            systems would be systems to evaluate capital
            investments, a target costing and value engineering
            system to manage the costs of new products and new
            product features, and monitoring systems to track R&D
            efforts;
          · quality management systems to control the quality of
            new product designs and the quality of production of
            existing products;
          · customer intelligence systems to gather data from the
            market on potential new features to include in new
            products, feedback on quality of existing products, and
            to get customer input on new product designs;

life-cycle cost management systems to control both prices and costs across the life cycle. Assuming that the originality of the Deere products is eventually matched by competitors such as Agco who can sell at lower prices, Deere may drop its products from the market earlier than its competitors.

c. It is easy to be skeptical of Ratliff's prediction. Although a strategy of following others' product innovations is likely to work for smaller competitors, it is unlikely to be as successful for the market leader.

    If Agco became the market leader under its present strategy, the incentives that Deere & Co. and the other current market leaders have to develop innovative products would be diminished and such companies may change their strategies to price-based competition to regain lost market share. In turn, the direct attack from the competitors would likely force Agco to become more innovative and compete more on its ability to differentiate its products from competitors.

43. The major problems in the Residential Products Division follow.
   - The mission of the division is not defined, nor is the broader strategy of the firm.
   - Ms. Green has no incentive to invest in assets that will foster future growth. Her compensation is a fixed salary and a bonus based on annual profit. The bonus scheme does not encourage growth. This is aggravated by the fact that Ms. Green is 53 years old and may be contemplating retirement in the not too distant future.
   - The division's growth is stagnant and market share is slipping. Further, the division does not seem to have a major presence in the growth sector of the market, ornamental products.
   - The division is not exploiting information technology. Although it has some computerized systems, apparently there is no integration of systems.
   - The division is obviously not customer focused. It has no customer service department and apparently no out-of-office sales staff to promote products.
   - The annual operating budget is the only major control tool that is used by upper management.

Some actions that could be taken to address the problems in the Residential Products Division follow.

- Develop a mission statement for the division that is consistent with the strategy of the firm. A strategic plan should also be compiled.

- Develop an integrated cost management system for the firm. The control systems need to be consistent with the strategy of the firm and the mission of the division. From the strong growth rate of the industry, some incentives need to be developed to encourage growth in market share and sales. Even if the mission is hold rather than grow, there is an opportunity for the division to regain lost market share.

- An integrated cost management system needs to be developed. The system should include incentive elements, reporting elements and informational elements. Informational elements should allow Ms. Green and other managers to obtain the information they need to make the division grow. For example, the division needs to develop the capability to determine what customers desire in garage door hardware and other products, the ability to monitor actions of competitors, and the necessary information to evaluate cost control efforts.

- Culturally and structurally, the division needs to become more customer focused. Structurally, the division can establish a customer service department and develop an external sales force to gather information from customers. Culturally, the division can become more customer focused by developing incentives for employees. Customer-related incentives could be based on measures of quality, lead time, product innovation, and customer service.

- Structurally, at the corporate level, the company may need to consider more decentralization of control. Using the operating budget as the only major control tool may place limits on actions that Ms. Green and her managers can take to improve operations. With decentralization of control, corporate management could develop new reporting elements for the cost management system that would facilitate growth in the Residential Products Division. For example, economic value added would be an excellent performance measure to encourage growth and customer focus.

Ethics and Quality Discussion
45. a.   The existence of a quality-oriented organization depends heavily on maintaining the trust of employees. When mistrust exists, introduction of any new initiatives that require the cooperation of employees will be difficult. To develop a corporate culture that embraces rather than fears change, managers must fiercely protect jobs of employees. If productivity increases lower the demand for employees, managers should use attrition rather than layoffs (to the extent possible) to reduce head count. To maintain full employment, managers can also redeploy displaced employees in divisions that are growing and are increasing headcount. Any quality initiatives that result in significant layoffs will drastically harm morale and may adversely affect quality. Therefore, managers must seriously consider whether such initiatives are worthwhile, and if so, what actions can be taken to minimize the adverse effects on employees.

     b.   Managers know that any illegal, dishonest, or immoral treatment of employees will generate negative consequences. An ethical treatment of employees would meet the following minimum criteria:
   · Any layoffs are in compliance with the law and not used as ruses to fire any particular subgroup of workers (e.g., senior workers, minorities).
   · Every effort should be made to help displaced workers find jobs in other firms or at other locations in the same company.
   · To the extent existing workers can be retrained for other positions in the firm, such training should be made available.
   · If the firm is successful and experiences future growth, new job opportunities should be first offered to displaced employees.
   · Managers should give employees as much notice as possible that layoffs are going to occur and who will be affected by them.

47. Because organizational culture can be an effective control tool, there is certainly an incentive to hire individuals who have a common culture. By hiring such individuals, a firm will increase the likelihood that all employees share common values and, therefore, will act in a predictable manner. Viewed in this light, diversity in the workforce is undesirable because it makes behavior less predictable. Allowing for a diverse workforce may require increased reliance on other existing control tools and the addition of more controls. From this point of view, there would appear to be no ethical problem in hiring workers who have a common culture. Only to the extent that culture is strongly associated with race, age, or other factors for which it is illegal to discriminate could ethical problems arise.

    However, there could be substantial negative consequences to hiring workers who are too homogeneous. Because the workers are so similar, they may have trouble relating to customers, suppliers, and others who subscribe to a different culture. Some diversity in values would provide more organizational knowledge for firms that have operations that span many countries, and have diverse customers and vendors. Additionally, if the common values of the culture are values that are not highly associated with success, an organization could be doomed to failure.

CHAPTER 3
OPERATING IN A QUALITY ENVIRONMENT

Questions

1. In the global economy, consumers have more choices than ever in buying products. To successfully position its products in this market, a company must maintain a reputation for delivering products of high quality and high perceived value. Accordingly, quality and value have emerged as important competitive dimensions in many markets. Competition based on these dimensions causes all competitors to strive to constantly deliver more value and higher quality at a lower price to maintain their shares of the market.

3. The eight characteristics are detailed in Exhibit 3-1. They are performance, features, reliability, conformance, durability, serviceability, aesthetics, and perceived quality.

5. Total quality management (TQM) is a philosophy of organizational management and change. At the center of the philosophy is the continuous improvement of the quality of all facets of operating the organization.
    Fundamental organizational change is required to implement TQM. Most organizations are adopting TQM after relying on inspection and monitoring to control the quality of operations; and quality control was the domain of some specific group in the organization. To adopt TQM, quality must become a foremost concern of all organizational participants. The organization must move from a philosophy of inspecting for defective work to a philosophy of building quality in. This requires a commitment from the entire organization, not just the management team.

7. Some customers simply demand more from an organization than they contribute. Such customers drain the capacity of the firm to serve more profitable clients. To better serve and retain the more profitable clients, a firm must be willing to "fire" marginal customers.

9. Employee empowerment refers to the assignment of responsibility and authority to employees to manage changes in their jobs. Additional costs that will be incurred include costs of training, and costs of bad decisions made by employees.

11. Benchmarking allows a firm to compare the quality of specific processes to the quality of firms that are viewed as excelling in such processes. By benchmarking the organization that is best at performing a given process, a firm can reasonably assess its relative quality in that process and identify specific actions that can be taken to subsequently improve the quality level.

13. The Baldrige Award is a recognition given by the Department of Commerce to U.S. firms achieving high levels of quality in their operations. The award categories are: Leadership, Strategic Planning, Customer and Market Focus, Information and Analysis, Human Resource Focus, Process Management, and Business Results.

15. The International Organization for Standardization was established as a cooperative effort of many countries to define process quality in business. This organization has issued five major pronouncements that set quality standards; these standards have been adopted by individual countries and, in part, by the European Union.

17. The four stages are (1) quality conformance, (2) quality consciousness, (3) quality competitive, and (4) quality culture. TQM is at the right of the continuum because it reflects a company that has achieved an organizational culture of continuous pursuit of quality improvement.

19. Pareto analysis helps identify the areas in which managers should focus their quality enhancement/cost reduction efforts so as to have the greatest impact. Managers can then allocate their time such that the amount of time invested in improving operations can be proportional to the benefits achieved.

21. Technology has influenced the processing of information in two ways. First, it has dramatically increased the power to process information. Technology has made it possible to process huge amounts of data in a very short time. Second, technology has reduced the cost of processing information. Cost reduction has been achieved by reducing the labor intensity of information processing.

Chapter 3
Operating in a Quality Environment

23. *Poka-yoke* are changes made to production systems or processes to make them more error proof. Examples include color coding forms so that one form cannot be confused with another; using a computer program that prompts the computer operator for information rather than asking the computer operator to enter data into blank electronic forms; and painting all of the components of a given product the same color so that a component of one product is not incorrectly made into a component of another product.

25. A flexible manufacturing system is one in which many or most of the machines are programmable, i.e., robotic. The major benefit of such machines is the speed with which they can be converted from the production of one product to another. The "setup" is computer controlled rather than manual.

Exercises

27. a. False. Adoption of TQM leads to continual change and improvement in production systems.

   b. False. Accounting practices need to evolve like all other business practices as technology and competitive conditions change.

   c. False. A focus on quality allows a firm to constantly change in response to new customer demands including demand for new products and product features.

   d. True.

   e. True.

   f. True.

   g. False. In benchmarking, a company will adopt only the practices of the benchmark firm that are appropriate given the firm's culture and competitive environment.

   h. True.

   i. False. Poor quality service causes a far greater loss of customers than do poor quality products.

Chapter 3
Operating in a Quality Environment

29. a. The important dimensions of the fuel include the intensity
         of the heat, the type and amount of emissions given off
         from burning the fuel, the ability of the fuel to burn in
         the existing facilities, and the reliability of the
         supply.

     b. The greatest concern would be related to the distance of
         the fuel from the power plant and the likelihood that
         weather or other transportation problems would interrupt
         the flow of coal to the plant.

     c. There is no single, correct answer to this question. The
         loss of the jobs at the Navasota Mining Company would
         occur in the backyard of the power plant. This would
         likely create political problems. It may have an affect
         on the morale of power plant employees as well. On the
         other hand, the power plant has an obligation to its
         customers to deliver electricity in the most economical
         manner possible; also, the power plant has an obligation
         to control pollution. The Wyoming fuel would clearly
         generate less pollution than the Texas fuel.

     d. Community goodwill and support of local employment.

Chapter 3
Operating in a Quality Environment

31. a.

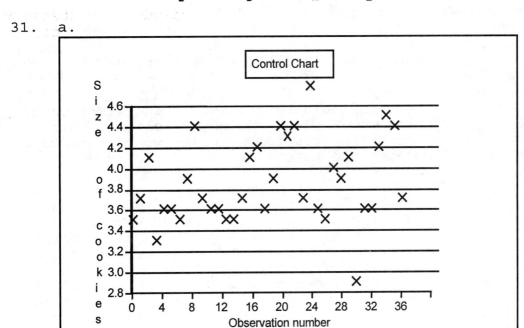

    b.   The control chart demonstrates that there is substantial variation in cookie size. Although, cookie size is concentrated around the 3.5 inch size, there are many cookies that are larger. If the objective is to stay in the range of 3.4 to 3.8 inches, this objective is not being achieved. It is also evident that the tendency is to err in the direction of making larger cookies.

33. a.   Costs of compliance include fitting machines for mistake-proof operations, supply-line management, and quality training. All others are costs of noncompliance.

    b.

	1999	2000	% change
Costs of compliance			
Fitting machines	$ 2,100	$ 3,200	+ 52
Educating suppliers	2,000	2,500	+ 25
Quality training	7,000	7,500	+ 7
Total	$11,100	$13,200	+ 19
Costs of noncompliance			
Customer refunds	$ 6,000	$ 4,500	- 25
Disposal of waste	11,000	9,000	- 18
Litigation claims	18,000	14,000	- 22
Total	$35,000	$27,500	- 21
Overall	$46,100	$40,700	- 12

c.   The pattern of change is consistent with quality-conscious management. The costs incurred for compliance have increased from 1999 to 2000 creating a favorable effect: a decrease in the costs of noncompliance. Thus, the company is spending more to prevent quality problems and spending less to treat quality problems.

35. a.   Cost to rework   140 X $14 = $1,960

b.   Lost profit from not reworking all defective units
         (240 - 140) X ($30 - $12) = $1,800

c.   Cost of processing customer returns
         25 X $18 = $450

d.   Total failure costs are the sum of the answers to a, b, and c.
         $1,960 + $1,800 + $450 = $4,210

e.
Total failure costs	$ 4,210
Prevention costs	10,000
Appraisal costs	12,000
Total quality cost	$26,210

37. a.   Your argument would be that private industry has used benchmarking to improve the quality of products and services and the processes that generate products and services. You might then pose the question as to why such a practice could not be adopted in government. Naturally, you would then answer the question: To the extent government units provide identifiable products or services to their constituencies, and have specific processes for doing so, they can benefit from benchmarking to the same extent as private industry.

b.   Politicians can strike a chord with voters by either outlining steps to improve the quality of services provided or by reducing taxes while maintaining a given level of services. Accordingly, you might argue that benchmarking will yield benefits in both reduced costs and increased quality of services. Costs may be reduced by eliminating wasted activities. Quality may be increased by improving internal processes.

Chapter 3
Operating in a Quality Environment

c. Hazards? What hazards? Well . . . there could be some risks, particularly in the area of results benchmarking. The main risk would be that the outcome measures would be pursued without due regard for the process. For example, to reduce teen pregnancies, the government might create programs that are unethical or too aggressive in dealing with pregnant teens; or, to improve the environment, the government might adopt regulations that strangle business in the state. Another risk is that the outcome measures will be manipulated to report progress toward the benchmarks although no real improvements have been made.

Problems

39. a. Price for good units: $270,000 ÷ $2,700 = $100
Price for defective units: $12,000 ÷ 300 = $40

Profits lost: 300 X ($100 - $40) = $18,000

b.
From selling defective units	$18,000
Rework costs	22,000
Total	$40,000

c.
Total failure costs	$40,000
Prevention and appraisal	45,000
Total	$85,000

d. The firm appears to be dedicated to the production of high quality products as evidenced by the relatively high spending for prevention and appraisal and the comparably low failure costs. Further, there were apparently no external failure costs.

Chapter 3
Operating in a Quality Environment

Cases

41. a. The biggest change to be noted is the customer focus. The first thing Mr. Lockhart did was to ask the presidents of the railroads what he could do for them. Another big change was the commitment to solve quality-related problems by redesigning components (*set up a task force of 100 engineers*). Also, Mr. Lockhart moved headquarters to the middle of the production facility. This signaled his commitment to production, his commitment to be involved in finding solutions to quality problems, and the importance of a quality product to the success of the locomotive division.

    b. Complacency is probably related to (1) the high barriers to entry in this industry, (2) the presence of only one major competitor, and (3) the fact that the main competitor had experienced substantial problems with quality in the recent past.

    c. The prescription for GM is the same as the one used by GE: focus on customers and meet their product requirements, build quality into the product design, and focus on eliminating wasted activities and decreasing cycle time.

    d. Product design is obviously the foundation of a quality product. A high quality design reduces the probability that there will be a need to inspect for quality problems, to deal with products that have failed in the customer applications, and to reengineer to solve problems that have been discovered after production.

Chapter 3
Operating in a Quality Environment

Ethics and Quality Discussions

43. a. The story suggests that the costs of "getting caught" in illegal behavior may well exceed the gains from engaging in such behavior.

     b. For government contractors, it may be reasonable for government to monitor compliance with both laws and internal ethical policies. Such monitoring would serve to assure the government that the business actually functions in a manner consistent with all control systems, including ethical policies. It is difficult to find a basis for government to monitor the ethical compliance of firms that do not contract with the government.

     c. The story suggests that in evaluating organizational control, it is just as important that managers gain assurance that operations are in compliance with internal ethical policies (an internal control mechanism) as to gain assurance that operations are legal (in compliance with externally imposed controls).

45. a. The purpose of asking this question is not to test the students' abilities to find the correct answer. There is none. Rather, the purpose is for the students to be able to identify the relevant issues. Considerations favoring hiring the disabled include allowing those with disabilities to constructively contribute their talents and services to government and industry, to allow for diversity in the workforce, to develop the technology that will allow disabled people to achieve in business, and for business to assume this important obligation in society—looking after the welfare of all citizens.

        On the other hand, an issue that should be considered is whether government has the right to force businesses to hire disabled people, particularly if hiring such individuals will cause the firm to be less competitive.

     b. Again, the authors offer no specific conclusion. The point is to discuss the vagueness of the term "reasonable" and what that term actually means in a given context.

Chapter 3
Operating in a Quality Environment

c.   Hiring disabled workers certainly will bring benefits: a favorable reputation, a more diverse workforce sensitive to the needs of disabled workers, the goodwill of the broader community, employees who may be uniquely qualified to perform certain tasks, and greater awareness of market opportunities available in serving the disabled.

Negative aspects of hiring disabled workers may include additional operating costs, possible inferior (less efficient) work performance, and more managerial time consumed by supervision and performance monitoring.

CHAPTER 4
COST TERMINOLOGY AND COST FLOWS

Questions

1. *Cost* is used to refer to so many different concepts that an adjective must be used to identify which particular concept of cost is being discussed. For example, there are fixed costs, period costs, expired costs, future costs, and opportunity costs.

3. A product cost is incurred to make or acquire inventory or to provide a service. In a manufacturing firm, product costs include direct materials, direct labor, and factory overhead. In a merchandising company, product costs are purchase costs plus freight-in. In a service company, service costs are primarily comprised of direct labor and overhead; direct materials are usually insignificant.

5. Manufacturing overhead has been growing most rapidly, because of the costs of technology. This cost category includes depreciation of factory and plant equipment, machinery maintenance cost, repair cost, some training costs, utilities expense to operate the machinery, and many costs related to quality control.

7. This statement is false. Prime cost consists of direct materials cost plus direct labor cost. Conversion cost is composed of the cost of direct labor and overhead. Therefore, the sum of the two would double-count the cost of direct labor and would not equal total product cost.

9. Because costs can only be expected to react in a consistent way as long as activity is within the relevant range. That is, only within the relevant range will variable costs remain constant per unit and fixed costs remain constant in total. If the company operates outside of the relevant range, assumptions about cost behavior are not valid and managers will need to reassess decisions which were based on prior assumptions about cost expectations.

11. A fixed cost remains constant, in total, across changes in the activity measure. A variable cost, in total, varies directly and proportionately with changes in the activity measure.

13. A step cost is a cost that remains constant, in total, across certain intervals of activity. Outside a given activity interval, the total cost changes. A step variable cost remains fixed only for very small activity intervals; a step fixed cost remains constant across wider intervals of activity.

15. This is necessary so that separate variable and fixed predetermined overhead rates can be prepared. If a combined predetermined rate is to be used, there is no need to separate mixed costs for product costing purposes. However, analysis of mixed costs may be done for purposes other than product costing.

17. A different fixed rate results at each different level of activity because fixed overhead is constant in total and varies inversely with changes in activity. In contrast, variable overhead is constant per unit of activity at all levels of activity within the relevant range. Because the fixed rate varies, management must choose one level by which to calculate a fixed rate that seems most reasonable for product costing. This results in uniformity in product costing. Since variable overhead is already constant per unit of activity at all levels within the relevant range, specifying the level of activity is unnecessary to determine the uniform predetermined variable overhead rate.

19. Some companies use multiple pools because there is no single allocation base that is the cost driver for overhead. This is the concept of a heterogeneous cost pool. The more and more diverse the set of costs in a given cost pool, the less likely it becomes that any single allocation base will bear a causal relationship to the cost pool. Consequently, by dividing the overhead cost pool into smaller pools, more homogeneous cost pools can be established, and these cost pools are more likely to be causally related to a single cost driver that can be used as an overhead allocation base.

21. Underapplication might be caused by lower than expected production levels, higher than normal fixed or variable costs, or an original low estimate of the amounts of estimated overhead costs. For fixed overhead, underapplication could also result from using theoretical or practical capacity as the denominator in computing the fixed overhead predetermined rate.

    If overhead were materially underapplied (or overapplied) for the year, the best method of handling the disposition of that amount is to allocate it to the accounts that contain applied overhead: work in process, finished goods, and cost of goods sold. However, a relatively small amount of underapplied overhead can be charged to cost of goods sold. If underapplied overhead is allocated in the manner described above, product costs and profits should be brought to their approximate actual levels with regard to overhead. In contrast, if a large amount of underapplied overhead were written off to cost of goods sold, then both product costs on the balance sheet and profits would be understated.

23. The Cost of Goods Manufactured is the cost of goods that were completed and available for sale during the current period. The Cost of Goods Sold is the cost of inventory sold during the period. The difference between the two amounts is equal to the change in the balance in finished goods inventory for the period.

25. A dependent variable is the variable of interest--the one to be explained or predicted. The independent variable is the explanatory variable, or the variable that is believed to cause or explain the variation in the dependent variable.

Exercises

27. a. DL
    b. OH
    c. DM
    d. DM
    e. DM
    f. DM
    g. DM
    h. OH
    i. DM or OH
    j. OH

Chapter 4
Cost Terminology and Cost Flows

29. a.
Total hours worked	7,000
Total regular hours worked	(5,000)
Overtime hours worked	2,000

   b.   To direct labor:
   7,000 hours × $8 = $56,000

   To overhead:
   $66,000 - $56,000 = $10,000

   c.   Shift premiums:
   Regular hours   2,500 × ($8 × .10) = $2,000
   Overtime premiums:
   2,000 hours × ($8 × .50) = $8,000

31. a. V, Product
    b. V, Product
    c. F, Period
    d. V, Product
    e. V, Product
    f. V, Product
    g. F Product
    h. F, Product (could be V if number of auditors varies with
                    volume)
    i. V, Product
    j. V, Product

33. a.
Direct materials	$ 718,000
Direct labor	421,000
Total prime cost	$1,139,000

   b.
Direct labor		$421,000
Overhead:		
Indirect materials	$102,000	
Indirect labor	129,000	
Factory utilities	103,000	334,000
Total conversion cost		$755,000

   c.
Direct materials	$718,000
Direct labor	421,000
Factory overhead	334,000
Total cost	$1,473,000

35. Fixed: $200   Variable: $.04 per page
    a.   1. $200 + ($.04 × 1,000) = $240
          2. $200 + ($.04 × 2,000) = $280
          3. $200 + ($.04 × 4,000) = $360

    b.   The total cost is increasing because there is a
          variable cost component; if all costs were fixed the
          answer would be the same in all three cases.

37. Cost of services rendered
    Direct labor:
Veterinary salaries	$23,000	
Assistant salaries	7,200	
Office salaries	1,700[a]	
Total direct labor		$31,900
Supplies		1,400[b]
Overhead:		
Utilities	$ 720	
Depreciation	2,100	
Building rental	1,360[c]	
Total overhead		$ 4,180
Cost of services rendered		$37,480

    [a] $3,400 × .50 = $1,700
    [b] $3,200 - $1,800 = $1,400
    [c] $1,700 × .80 = $1,360

39. a. Maintenance expense = a + bX
        $$b = \frac{\$600 - \$150}{\$60,000-\$30,000} = \frac{\$450}{\$30,000} = \$0.015$$

        a = $600 - ($0.015 × 60,000)
          = $600 - $900
          = $(300)
        Budget formula: Y = $(300) + $0.015X

    b. The improbable result is the negative fixed cost.
        Costs cannot be negative unless there is some unusual
        subsidy involved. The likely reasons for the negative
        intercept are that one of the data points used was
        anomalous (an outlier), there is an error in the data,
        or one of the observations is outside of the relevant
        range.

41. a.   **CD sales volume**

	5,000	7,000	9,000
Total VC	$9,250	$12,950	$15,750
VC per CD	$1.85	$1.85	$1.75
Total FC	$3,500	$ 5,200	$ 5,200
FC per CD	.70	.74	.58
Total cost	$12,750	$18,150	$20,950

  b. Total cost
      per CD $2.55 $2.59 $2.33

43. a.   1. VOH rate = $44,000 ÷ 11,000 = $4.00 per MH
           FOH rate = $15,000 ÷ 11,000 = $1.36 per MH

      2. Products = 11,000 ÷ 2 = 5,500
          VOH rate = $44,000 ÷ 5,500 = $8.00 per unit
          FOH rate = $15,000 ÷ 5,500 = $2.73 per unit

  b.   1. OH rate = ($44,000 + $15,000) ÷ 11,000
               = $5.36 per MH
      2. OH rate = $59,000 ÷ 5,500 = $10.73 per unit

  c.   1. Applied FOH = 884 × 1.36 = $1,202.24
      2. Applied VOH = 884 × 4.00 = $3,536
      3. $3,536 - $3,360 = $176 overapplied variable
                         overhead

          $1,202.24 - $1,310.00 = $(107.76) underapplied
                                   fixed overhead
          $176 overapplied VOH - $107.76 underapplied FOH
                    = $68.24 overapplied combined overhead

45. a.   OH rate = $60,000 ÷ 10,000 hours = $6.00 per DL hour

  b.   Labor = 1,430 hrs. × $4.50 per hr = $6,435
      Applied OH = 1,430 hrs. × $6.00 per hr = $8,580
      Material = $17,500 - $6,435 - $8,580 = $2,485

  c. $60,000 - $61,350 = $1,350 underapplied

47. a.   WIP: $ 27,000 $31,000 × 27/300   = $2,790
          FG: 60,000   31,000 × 60/300   = $6,200
          CGS: _213,000_   31,000 × 213/300   = $22,010
          Total $300,000

          (1)   Manufacturing OH   31,000
                    WIP   2,790
                    FG inventory   6,200
                    COGS   22,010
          (2)   Manufacturing OH   31,000
                    COGS   31,000

     b.   The allocation under part a.(1) is better, because it
          more nearly matches the costs that would be assigned
          under an actual costing system.

49. a.   Determining the cost of a product merely involves
          tracing direct costs to production and finding some
          systematic method of allocating indirect production
          costs to the products. Controlling these costs
          involves completely different issues. Control of
          production costs requires a focus on both the product
          costs and the related cost drivers. Such costs can
          only be controlled by controlling the activity levels
          of the main production cost drivers.

     b.   The advancement of technology does make costs more
          difficult to control. As technology has become more
          pervasive in manufacturing, the indirect manufacturing
          costs have grown relative to the direct manufacturing
          costs. Many of these new indirect product costs are
          fixed relative to production volume. Hence, merely
          controlling production volume has little to do with the
          control of more and more production costs. Further,
          with the growth in the indirect costs, it is more
          difficult to trace production costs to specific
          products. This adds to the complexity of cost control
          because the relationship between production volume of
          specific products and product costs is less obvious.

     c.   Production volume is no longer as significant a cost
          driver as it was a few years ago. Both the growth in
          fixed costs and the growth in indirect costs suggests
          that production volume cannot be used as an effective
          control for a substantial set of production-related
          costs. However, it may still be a valid cost predictor
          because it may be reasonably well correlated with the
          actual cost drivers of these indirect costs and it is
          still the most significant cost driver for direct
          production costs.

Chapter 4
Cost Terminology and Cost Flows

Problems

51. 1. D
    2. K
    3. I
    4. A
    5. G
    6. C
    7. B
    8. F
    9. L

53. a. Variable cost for 1,000 dinners
= $900 + $360 + $120 + $950 = $\underline{\$2,330}$ ÷ 1,000 dinners

Total cost = $1,200,000 + $2,330 × 300 = $1,899,000
$1,899,000 ÷ 300,000 = $\underline{\$6.33}$ cost per dinner based on average sales and April prices

b. Total costs = $1,200,000 + $2,330 × 400 = $2,132,000
$2,132,000 ÷ 400,000 = $\underline{\$5.33}$ cost per dinner

c. Total costs = $6.33 × 400,000 = $2,532,000
$1,200,000 + (? × 400) = $2,532,000
? × 400 = $1,332,000
? = $3,330

$3,330 - $950 - $120 - $360 = $\underline{\$1,900}$
$1,900 ÷ 1,000 = $\underline{\$1.90}$ allowable cost of meat per meal

d. Target cost per dinner = $10.96 ÷ 2 = $\underline{\$5.48}$

Total cost = $1,200,000 + $2,330 × Q

Total cost ÷ 1,000Q = $5.48
Total cost = $5,480Q

Using substitution:
$5,480Q = $1,200,000 + $2,330Q
$3,150Q = $1,200,000
Q = 380.952
380.952 × 1000 = $\underline{380,952}$ dinners

55. a.   Direct materials = $16,900 + $90,000 - $21,700
                            = $85,200
          Direct labor = 6,800 × $9 = $61,200

          Prime costs = $85,200 + $61,200 = $146,400

     b.   Conversion = $61,200 + $109,300 = $170,500

     c.   Beginning bal., work in process, 5/1 $ 32,100
          Manufacturing costs:
            Direct materials $ 85,200
            Direct labor   61,200
            Overhead   109,300
          Total manufacturing costs   255,700
          Total costs to account for $287,800
          Ending bal., work in process, 5/31   29,600
          Cost of goods manufactured $258,200

     d.   Beginning bal., finished goods, 5/1 $ 25,800
          Cost of goods manufactured   258,200
          Cost of goods available for sale   284,000
          Ending bal., finished goods, 5/31   22,600
          Cost of goods sold $261,400

57. a.   Overhead = $69,400 + $12,350[a] + 45,400[b] = $127,150
          [a] $95,000 × .13 = $12,350 indirect labor
          [b] $18,000 + $92,000 - $16,700 = $93,300 raw materials
               used
            $93,300 raw materials used - $47,900 direct materials
             = $45,400 indirect materials cost

     b.   Beg. bal., work in process, 7/1 $ 24,500
          Manufacturing costs:
            Direct material $ 47,900
            Direct labor   82,650
            Overhead   127,150
          Total manufacturing costs   257,700
          Total costs to account for $282,200
          Ending bal., work in process, 7/31   19,200
          Cost of goods manufactured $263,000

     c.   Beg. bal., finished goods, 7/1 $ 8,000
          Cost of goods manufactured   263,000
          Cost of goods available for sale $271,000
          Ending bal., finished goods, 7/31   9,200
          Cost of goods sold $261,800

59.

	Case #1	Case #2	Case #3
Sales	$9,300	19,700[k]	$112,000
Direct materials used	1,200	6,100[h]	18,200
Direct labor	2,500[a]	4,900	32,100[m]
Prime cost	3,700	11,000[i]	50,300[n]
Conversion cost	4,800	8,200	49,300
Overhead	2,300[b]	3,300[g]	17,200
Cost of goods manufactured	6,200	14,000	68,900[o]
Beg. work in process	500	900	5,600
Ending work in process	300[c]	1,200	4,200
Beginning finished goods	800[e]	1,900	7,600
Ending finished goods	1,200	3,700[l]	4,300[p]
Cost of goods sold	5,800[d]	12,200	72,200
Gross profit	3,500	7,500[j]	39,800[q]
Operating expenses	1,300[f]	3,500	18,000
Net income (loss)	2,200	4,000	21,800[r]

[a] $3,700 - 1,200 = 2,500$
[b] $4,800 - 2,500 = 2,300$
[c] $500 + 1,200 + 2,500 + 2,300 - 6,200 = 300$
[d] $9,300 - 3,500 = 5,800$
[e] $5,800 - 6,200 + 1,200 = 800$
[f] $3,500 - 2,200 = 1,300$
[g] $8,200 - 4,900 = 3,300$
[h] $14,000 + 1,200 - 900 - 8,200 = 6,100$
[i] $6,100 + 4,900 = 11,000$
[j] $4,000 + 3,500 = 7,500$
[k] $12,200 + 7,500 = 19,700$
[l] $1,900 + 14,000 - 12,200 = 3,700$
[m] $49,300 - 17,200 = 32,100$
[n] $18,200 + 32,100 = 50,300$
[o] $18,200 + 32,100 + 17,200 + 5,600 - 4,200 = 68,900$
[p] $7,600 + 68,900 - 72,200 = 4,300$
[q] $112,000 - 72,200 = 39,800$
[r] $39,800 - 18,000 = 21,800$

61. a. **Framing:** **Covering:**

a = $4,200   a = $3,000
b = $6,600 ÷ 3,000 = $2.20 b = $45,000 ÷ 9,000 = $5.00

b. 6,000 sofas => 6,000 MHs => 18,000 DLHs
Framing OH: $4,200 + ($2.20 × 6,000) = $17,400
Covering OH: $3,000 + ($5.00 × 18,000) = $93,000

c. Normal: $\dfrac{\$78,000^* + \$15,200^*}{5,000}$ = $18.64 per sofa

Expected: $\dfrac{\$93,000 + \$17,400}{6,000}$ = $18.40 per sofa

*From flexible budget at the normal capacity level of 5,000 DLH.

d. Expected capacity should be used. If normal capacity is used, actual gross margin will be less than 50 percent of product cost because actual volume will be below the volume level used to determine the cost estimates, i.e., fixed overhead cost per unit will be above the estimated amount.

63. a.
Increase in RM inventory	$ 20,000
RM used	400,000
RM purchased	$420,000

b.
Increase in WIP	$ 60,000
Cost of Goods Manufactured	800,000
WIP cost to account for	$860,000

$860,000 - $400,000 = $460,000
        RM used   DL & MOH

$460,000 = X + .60X
$460,000 = 1.60X
$287,500 = X = Direct Labor Cost

c. 287,500 × .60 = $172,500

d. $200,000 + $800,000 - X = $170,000
$200,000 + $800,000 - $170,000 = X
$830,000 = X = COGS

e. $900,000 - $830,000 - $140,000 = $(70,000)

Cases

65. a. Direct labor is labor that can be specifically identified with, or physically traced to, a cost object or finished product in an economically feasible manner (e.g., the labor of machine operators in a production environment). Indirect labor is all factory labor that is not classified as direct labor.

b. Certain nonproductive time may be a normal and unavoidable part of total labor time. In such cases, a pro rata share of nonproductive time should be classified as direct labor time. In many cases, nonproductive time is classified as indirect labor because it cannot be specifically identified with a cost object. For example, the amount of downtime usually cannot be specifically identified with a specific cause or particular cost object; it may result from a parts shortage or a broken machine. Similarly, training may be a fill-in for a shortage of work.

Chapter 4
Cost Terminology and Cost Flows

c. **Direct labor** The items classified as direct labor can usually be specifically identified with a quantity of labor. Furthermore, other direct costs, such as payroll taxes, are incurred by the organization because of its utilization of quantities of labor.

Manufacturing overhead The items classified as manufacturing overhead usually cannot be specifically identified with direct labor quantities.

Either direct labor or manufacturing overhead Some cost items may be classified as either direct labor or manufacturing overhead, depending on the size of the cost object. For very large projects, for example, employees can be easily identified with the projects (e.g., managers, engineers, draftspersons, janitors, material handlers). Therefore, all costs associated with these employees may be classified as direct labor costs. For smaller costs objects, such as a variety of products or subassemblies, costs are more difficult to identify with cost objects and, therefore, they are classified as manufacturing overhead.

d. The quantity of labor hours that should be included as direct labor or manufacturing overhead reflects a measure of activity. The activity that was performed was either directly related to the product or indirectly related (or not easily traceable) to the product. The dollar amount assigned measures the cost of the activity. For example, a direct labor employee makes $8 per hour and time-and-a-half for overtime. This employee's activity is no different during the overtime hours--only his wage rate is different. Thus, the measurement of activity and measurement of cost must be separated.

(CMA adapted)

67. a. Alan Shane's perception of Susan Brady is not positive although he does not openly criticize her. He sees her as an agent of corporate headquarters who is unwilling to change or request top management to make changes in the reporting requirements. Shane sees Brady as an accountant who does not understand the production aspects of the organization.

   b. Alan Shane perceives corporate headquarters as unfair in that they are using only the cost report to judge performance thereby ignoring product quality, employee pride, and employee motivation. He also feels headquarters lacks understanding of his operations and that they are out of touch with current operations.
      Shane believes the cost report is useless and biased because it is inflexible and not subject to the changing conditions of a production process. The report also fails to recognize achievements and highlights only operational shortcomings.

   c. Shane perceives himself as a qualified production manager who is interested in manufacturing a quality product at minimum cost. However, Shane is frustrated that he is unable to get satisfactory cooperation from the Accounting Department or top management. He sees himself as a victim of corporate gameplaying; he finds himself in a no-win situation no matter how good he is as a production manager.

   d. At least three changes could be made:
      1. Use a flexible budget rather than a static master budget for measuring performance. This allows for separate analysis of fixed and variable costs and provides a control for fluctuations in volume.
      2. Use standard costs rather than actual costs.
      3. Separate controllable costs from noncontrollable costs for performance evaluation purposes and clearly identify those elements of the operation for which the production manager is directly responsible.

                                                            (CMA)

Ethics and Quality Discussion
69. a.   Overhead costs would be the easiest to assign to other
          classifications since they are not directly related to
          the production of the goods.

     b.   Consider the following: the reason for the bank's loan-
          granting criteria; the effect on other bank customers
          should this company's loan be granted; the effect on
          the company's suppliers, employees, and customers
          should this loan not be granted; and the ability to
          manipulate financial income.

     c.   The memo should contain information as to the nature of
          costs and the fact that the "cost" of a product can, in
          many instances, have many different meanings. It should
          indicate the need for the loan, the ability to provide
          collateral (if any), and provide information as to
          payback. The memo should indicate that the "bottom
          line" is in excess of the bank's criteria and how this
          fact could influence the ability to repay. Cash flow
          from product sales should also be discussed, because
          without cash flow, income cannot pay back loans.

71.   a.   Society demands that hospitals sometimes treat patients who can't pay for their services. Bad debts also occur in commercial businesses because some customers can't or won't pay. In both cases, paying customers are affected by the costs resulting from nonpaying customers. The difference is that the hospital *knowingly* provides free services to nonpaying customers based on the belief that society expects this.

   b.   Other costs include depreciation of plant and equipment, new and special equipment costs, research, continuing education of personnel, salaries of top administrators of the hospital, costs of marketing the hospital, and other costs.

   c.   If the community, as a matter of public policy, considers it appropriate for hospitals to conduct a certain amount of indigent and other nonpaying care, then it seems logically consistent to include these costs in the overhead rate.

   d.   As paying customers, most patients probably find $7 aspirin unpalatable at first. However, assuming that the paying customer can accept the validity of the costs and their magnitudes included in the charge, he or she may conclude that if the costs aren't added to the aspirin charge, they will be added elsewhere. If any organization is to survive in its present mode, its pricing must cause revenues to equal or exceed costs in the long run. The hospital manager will, no doubt, take this position. The hospital manager is not paying the hospital bill and his/her motivation is to defend the concept of covering all costs through fair and equitable hospital pricing practices.

Chapter 4
Cost Terminology and Cost Flows

CHAPTER 5
ACTIVITY-BASED MANAGEMENT

Questions

1. Product cost information is necessary to allow managers to accomplish two requirements: (1) financial reporting of inventories and cost of goods sold; and (2) effective and efficient conduct of the managerial functions of planning, controlling, evaluating, and decision making (such as pricing).

3. It is not possible to develop totally accurate product or service costs because all costs cannot be traced directly to products or services. Although more costs are being traced through machine counters and bar code scanners, some costs (such as supervisors' salaries) will always be indirect to products or services.

5. A process map sequentially depicts all of the steps associated with accomplishing a specific task. Most process maps are drawn as flowcharts. By carefully studying the steps, value-added and non-value-added activities can be identified and ideas can be generated to reduce or eliminate the non-value-added activities.

7. Value-added activities increase the worth of a product or service to the consumer. Non-value-added activities increase the time spent on a product or service but do not increase its worth. Performing tasks required for production (adding materials, blending, molding, assembling, and so forth) are value-added activities; moving partially completed units of inventory, storing parts, inspecting for quality, and allowing parts to sit and wait to be worked on are examples of non-value-added activities.

9. Non-value-added activities can be attributed to systemic, physical, and human factors. These factors, which are unique to individual producers or service providers, add no market value or quality to the product so the customer would perceive them as non-value-added.

49

11.   Cycle efficiency measures operational efficiency. In a manufacturing environment, cycle efficiency is calculated as value-added processing time divided by total cycle time. The numerator refers to the actual time it takes to physically manufacture a unit. Total cycle time is value-added time plus all time spent on non-value-added activities, such as inspection time, transfer time, and idle time. In an optimized manufacturing environment, the non-value-added activities would be eliminated so the value of the MCE would be 100 percent.

     In a service environment, cycle efficiency is calculated as value-added service time divided by total cycle time. The numerator refers to the actual time it takes to physically manufacture a unit. Total cycle time is the time from the placement of a service order to service completion.

13.   Yes, cost drivers exist in conventional accounting systems although they are generally called *allocation bases*. In conventional systems, a single cost driver such as direct labor hours or machine hours is commonly used rather than multiple cost drivers. Also in conventional systems, volume-based cost drivers are more the norm than non-volume-based cost drivers, such as square footage. Finally, conventional accounting stresses finding an allocation base that demonstrates strong statistical correlation to the cost, but ABC emphasizes searching for multiple cost drivers that bear cause-and-effect relationships to the cost.

15.   The four levels of cost drivers are unit, batch, product/process, and organizational/facility. The traditional costing system focuses on variable costs and assumes that these are all incurred at the unit level. Activity-based costing requires costs to be aggregated at different levels because the activities that cause costs to be generated occur at different levels. Only if costs are accumulated on the same level as the activity that generates them can an allocation base be selected that represents a cause-effect relationship between the cost and the cost pool.

17.   By using a single cost pool and a single cost driver to allocate overhead, the more traditional methods of overhead assignment ignore the influence on cost of the different activities that occur to make a product. In this manner, low-volume specialty products, which cause a disproportionate amount of overhead, are assigned only an average charge for overhead, thereby shifting costs to the standard product lines. ABC does a better job of tracing costs to the products that caused such costs by using multiple cost pools and multiple cost drivers.

19. Visible reflections of dysfunctional cost systems are
     managers' dissatisfaction that cost information is (a) too
     late to be of use in controlling and problem solving; (b)
     inaccurate and distorted, leading to poor management
     decisions; (c) inadequate in providing managers with an
     ability to compete with confidence; and (d) not believable.

21. There are four primary methods of mass customization.
     Collaborative customizers work with individual customers to
     determine needs. An example of this type would be a caterer
     for a wedding. Adaptive customizers allow customers to adapt
     a standard product for their own needs. For example, some
     Sears' garage door openers can be adapted to customer needs
     to open different doors or to turn on house lights. Cosmetic
     customizers make a standard product with different "looks"
     for different customers. For example, a chocolate
     manufacturer may package standard chocolates under the names
     of different stores. Transparent customizers give customers
     unique goods or services without letting them know that those
     products or services have been customized for them. For
     example, a company that makes hand lotion may tint or scent
     that lotion differently for different purchasers (such as
     Marriott or Delta Air Lines).

23. In ABC, control is exerted on the cause of a cost which is
     the activity and its cost driver, whereas in conventional
     costing, control is focused on the cost itself. Control of
     the source of a cost is the more effective way to control
     the cost. This is analogous to treating the cause, rather
     than the symptoms, of an illness.

25. ABC is not widely used for cost assignment in external
     reporting because (a) the new costs would not significantly
     affect income or assets; (b) the system is not used firm-
     wide and, thus, makes internal comparisons difficult; and
     (c) the new costs may not be fully consistent with generally
     accepted accounting principles or Internal Revenue Service
     regulations.

27. Yes, some firms are likely to benefit more than others from
     adopting ABC. These firms would recognize that the benefits
     of the improved information substantially exceed the costs
     of implementation. Such firms are those that produce
     multiple products or services, have some products or
     services that are more complex to produce than others, have
     a wide variation in volume across product/service lines,
     rely heavily on cost information to make decisions, have
     multiple cost drivers, face an uncertain and changing
     environment, and have little faith in cost allocations under
     the existing system.

29. This statement is not true. Activity-based costing, in and of itself, is merely a different overhead allocation mechanism. Costs are not removed but rather reassigned and profits will remain the same or decrease because of the implementation of ABC.

Exercises

31.
a.	10	f.	7
b.	9	g.	1
c.	8	h.	6
d.	2	i.	4
e.	3	j.	5

33. a. Value-added activities add value to the clients.
   - Take depositions
   - Do legal research
   - Litigate case
   - Write correspondence, if necessary to litigation strategy or results in desired action for the client
   - Contemplate litigation strategies, if enhances ideas and results in better litigation
   - Write wills

   b. Non-value-added activities are non-essential to client work.
   - Travel to/from court
   - Eat lunch with clients, unless discussion relates to case and results in something of value
   - Eat dinner at office while watching Jeopardy
   - Play golf
   - Assign tasks to the firm secretary (may be business-value-added)
   - Fill out time sheets for client work (is business-value-added)

   c. A large law firm probably has paralegals and associates to perform some of the above-mentioned tasks as well as other non-value-added activities that were not mentioned. For instance, there may be someone in a large firm to drive the attorneys to court so that they can use the time for other value-added activities.

35. a. None of the items are value-added activities; products should be designed so that schedule changes are not needed.

   b. The cost driver is number of factory schedule changes.

   c. The plant manager needs to do a better job of planning so that factory schedule changes are eliminated except those requested by a customer (who should then be charged for the cost of the change) or those that are necessary for significant quality improvements and cost reductions.

37. Each student will have different answers. No solution provided.

39. a.

Receiving ingredients (NVA)	45
Moving ingredients to stockroom (NVA)	15
Storing ingredients in stockroom (NVA)	7,200
Moving ingredients from stockroom (NVA)	15
Mixing ingredients (VA)	50
Cooking ingredients (VA)	185
Bottling ingredients (VA)	90
Moving bottled sauce to warehouse (NVA)	20
Storing bottled sauce in warehouse (NVA)	10,080
Moving bottled sauce from warehouse to trucks (NVA)	30

b. Cycle time = 45 + 15 + 7,200 + 15 + 50 + 185 + 90 + 20 + 10,080 + 30 = <u>17,730</u>

MCE = (50 + 185 + 90) ÷ 17,730 = .002

c. Mr. Logan might consider a just-in-time inventory purchasing and production system. His longest times are in storage on the front and back end of the production process and in moving the goods in and out of storage. He also may want to negotiate some long-term contracts with his customers so that he has a better idea of when they will want what quantities of his sauce.

41. a. number of pizzas cooked
b. number of deliveries made, number of miles driven, age of drivers
c. age of building, type of construction
d. number of side orders, proportion of number of pizzas
e. value of building, location of building
f. number of miles driven, average miles per hour

43. a. Cost of printing books at a publishing house (B)
b. Cost of preparing payroll checks (B)
c. Cost of supplies used in research and development on an existing product (P)
d. Salary of the Vice-President of Marketing (O)
e. Cost of developing an engineering change order (P)
f. Depreciation on camera at Drivers' License Office in the Department of Motor Vehicles (P)
g. Salary of guard for 5-story headquarters building (O)
h. Cost of paper and cover for a passport (U)

45. a. $450,000 ÷ 150,000 calls = $3 per call
$150,000 ÷ 10,000 purchase orders = $15 per purchase order
$110,250 ÷ 7,000 receiving reports = $15.75 per receiving report
Cost assignment:

118 calls × $3	$ 354
37 purchase orders × $15	555
28 receiving reports × $15.75	441
Total	$1,350

   b. $1,350 ÷ 200 units = $6.75 per unit

   c. $3 × .75 = $2.25 per call
$15 × .75 = $11.25 per purchase order
$15.75 × .75 = $11.81 per receiving report
Cost assignment:

20 calls × $2.25	$ 45.00
15 purchase orders × $11.25	168.75
8 receiving reports × $11.81	94.48
Total	$308.23 ÷ 200 = $1.54

47. a. Overhead: $13,200,000 ÷ 55,000 DLHs = $240 per DLH

	Plastic Bottles	Control Panels
Revenue	$6,000,000	$13,000,000
Direct material	(1,360,000)	(1,200,000)
Direct labor	(28,000)a	(742,000)b
Overhead	(480,000)	(12,720,000)
Profit (loss)	$4,132,000	$(1,662,000)

   a $240 × 2,000 = $480,000
   b $240 × 53,000 = $12,720,000

   b. Overhead: $13,200,000 ÷ 206,250 MHs = $64 per MH

	Plastic Bottles	Control Panels
Revenue	$ 6,000,000	$13,000,000
Direct material	(1,360,000)	(1,200,000)
Direct labor	(28,000)a	(742,000)b
Overhead	(7,680,000)	(5,520,000)
Profit (loss)	$(3,068,000)	$5,538,000

   a $64 × 120,000 = $7,680,000
   b $64 × 86,250 = $5,520,000

c. Overhead: $9,500,000 ÷ 55,000 DLHs = $173 per DLH
    $2,500,000 ÷ 206,250 MHs = $12 per MH
    $1,200,000 ÷ $19,000,000 = $.06 per revenue $

	Plastic Bottles	Control Panels
Revenue	$6,000,000	$13,000,000
Direct material	(1,360,000)	(1,200,000)
Direct labor	(28,000) a	(742,000) b
Overhead	(2,146,000)	(10,984,000)
Profit	$2,466,000	$ 74,000

a ($173 × 2,000) + ($12 × 120,000) + ($.06 ×
    $6,000,000)
b = $346,000 + $1,440,000 + $$360,000 = $2,146,000
    ($173 × 53,000) + ($12 × 86,250) + ($.06 ×
    $13,000,000)
    = $9,169,000 + $1,035,000 + $780,000 = $10,984,000

d. Overhead: $9,500,000 ÷ 55,000 DLHs = $173 per DLH
    $2,500,000 ÷ 206,250 MHs = $12 per MH

	Plastic Bottles	Control Panels	Total
Revenue	$6,000,000	$13,000,000	$19,000,000
DM	(1,360,000)	(1,200,000)	(2,560,000)
DL	(28,000) a	(742,000) b	(770,000)
OH	(1,786,000)	(10,204,000)	(11,990,000)
Profit	$2,826,000	$ 854,000	$ 3,680,000
Admin. OH			(1,200,000)
Profit			$ 2,480,000

a ($173 × 2,000) + ($12 × 120,000) = $346,000 +
b $1,440,000 = $1,786,000
    ($173 × 53,000) + ($12 × 86,250) = $9,169,000 +
       $1,035,000 = $10,204,000

e. The solution in Part d best reflects the profit
    generated by each product because overhead costs are
    assigned using a related cost driver. Neither product
    is burdened with overhead truly caused by the other.
    And, unless there is some cause-effect relationship
    between administrative overhead costs and revenue
    dollars, it is best to deduct these from total product
    line contribution.

Problems

49. a.   Value-added activities:

Stripping the road	10
Laying asphalt on the road	5
Total VA time	15 hours

      b.   Non-value-added activities:

Driving to the work location	1
Blocking off the road	2
Setting up the road stripper	3
Drinking coffee	13
Setting up the asphalt layer	7
Talking to each other	4
Unblocking the road	3
Loading equipment and leaving area	2
Total NVA time	35 hours

      c.   Cycle efficiency = 15 ÷ 50 = <u>30 percent</u>
This result indicates that 70 percent of the time is adding costs, but no value, to the customer (the NYC resident). An easy way to increase cycle efficiency would be to eliminate 17 hours of coffee-drinking and talking time; this would bring cycle efficiency up to 45 percent (15 ÷ 33). Possibly better training could reduce some of the other NVA times.

51. a.   Use the high-low method to determine the variable and fixed cost portions: $6,200 - $5,000 = $1,200; $1,200 ÷ (22 - 10) = $1,200 ÷ 12 = $100 variable cost; $5,000 - ($100 × 10) = $4,000 fixed cost

           Variable purchasing costs would include supplies, long-distance telephone calls, postage, and equipment maintenance. Fixed purchasing costs would include purchasing agent's and secretary's salaries, depreciation on floor space and equipment, rental charges or flat monthly fee for telephone and utilities.

      b.   The number of machine setups could have increased by 14 for the following reasons: (1) all parts of the special orders were not run at the same time; (2) desk sizes could have differed substantially; (3) desks may have needed rework after quality inspections; or (4) special orders could have been interspersed with production of regular desks.

      c.   The cost of quality control and inspections could have increased because (1) special orders may be inspected more carefully or more often than regular orders or (2) special orders may all be inspected rather than the random selection of regular orders.

d. Engineering design and specification costs were not
    included in the original list of overhead costs because
    that list pertained only to regular production. It is
    only when special orders are obtained that new designs
    and specifications need to be developed.

e. Purchasing cost: number of purchase orders
    Machine setup: number of different types of production;
        number of setups
    Utilities: number of machine hours
    Supervisors: number of supervisors; number of direct
        labor hours, number of production workers
    Depreciation: period of time
    Quality control and inspection: number of desks
        inspected; hours of quality control time; machine
        hours
    Engineering design and specification: number of special
        orders accepted; hours of design time

f. No. First, the method used did not consider additional
    costs such as engineering. Second, the method used
    failed to discriminate in costing between the regular
    and the special orders. ABC would overcome these
    deficiencies.

53. a. Predetermined rate using machine hours: $7,200,000 ÷
        1,200,000 MHs = $6 per MH

    b. Direct material $120,000
        Direct labor   360,000
        Applied overhead ($6 × 12,000 MHs)   72,000
        Total cost $552,000
        Divided by number of doors   ÷ 5,000
        Cost per door $110.40

c. Predetermined rate per activity per unit of cost
    driver:
    Electric power: $600,000 ÷ 120,000 = $5 per kwh
    Work cells: $3,600,000 ÷ 720,000 = $5 per square foot
    Materials handling: $1,200,000 ÷ 240,000 = $5 per
        move
    Quality Control: $1,200,000 ÷ 120,000 = $10 per
        inspection
    Product Runs: $600,000 ÷ 60,000 = $10 per run

Direct material		$120,000
Direct labor		360,000
Applied overhead		
Electric power ($5 × 1,200)	$ 6,000	
Work cells ($5 × 9,600)	48,000	
Materials handling ($5 × 120)	600	
Quality control ($10 × 60)	600	
Product runs ($10 × 30)	300	55,500
Total cost		$535,500
Divided by number of doors		÷ 5,000
Cost per door		$107.10

d. The activity-based costing method allocates the cost
    pools of manufacturing overhead to various cost drivers
    and then to products based on quantity of the various
    cost drivers that each product consumes. Assume that
    Beaver Window's policy is to add 40 percent to
    manufacturing costs as gross profit to cover expenses
    such as administrative, selling, financial, and
    research and development; the remainder will be a
    profit. In determining the selling price of the window
    under both methods, add 40 percent of total
    manufacturing costs:

	Present Costing System	ABC System
Unit costs	$110.40	$107.10
40% gross profit	44.16	42.84
Selling price	$154.56	$149.94

It is evident that a selling advantage results from the
ABC method. As illustrated in this case, the ABC method
should result in a pricing decision that makes the
company more competitive in the marketplace. Savings in
applying manufacturing overhead costs to products will
enable the company to sell its products at a lower
price than competitors while maintaining the same gross
margin ratio.

[Copyright 1990 IMA (formerly NAA)]

55. a. $1,551,000 ÷ (20,000 + 25,000) = $1,551,000 ÷ 45,000 =
        $34.47 per DLH
      Cost per pound of material = $363,000 ÷ 220,000 = $1.65

Product A

Direct material (93,000 × $1.65)	$ 153,450
Direct labor (20,000 × $12)	240,000
Overhead (20,000 × $34.47)	689,400
Total cost	$1,082,850
Divided by number of units	÷ 10,000
Cost per unit	$108.29

Product B

Direct material (127,000 × $1.65)	$ 209,550
Direct labor (25,000 × $12)	300,000
Overhead (25,000 × $34.47)	861,750
Total cost	$1,371,300
Divided by number of units	÷ 5,000
Cost per unit	$274.26

  b. $1,551,000 ÷ (35,000 + 15,000) = $1,551,000 ÷ 50,000 =
        $31.02 per MH

Product A

Direct material	$ 153,450
Direct labor	240,000
Overhead (35,000 × $31.02)	1,085,700
Total cost	$1,479,150
Divided by number of units	÷ 10,000
Cost per unit	$147.92

Product B

Direct material	$209,550
Direct labor	300,000
Overhead (15,000 × $31.02)	465,300
Total cost	$974,850
Divided by number of units	÷ 5,000
Cost per unit	$194.97

c.   Allocation rates:
        Utilities ($500,000 ÷ 50,000) $10 per MH
        Setup ($105,000 ÷ 700) $150 per setup
        Material handling ($946,000 ÷ 220,000) $4.30 per pound

Product A

Direct material	$ 153,450
Direct labor	240,000
Utilities overhead (35,000 × $10)	350,000
Setup overhead (200 × $150)	30,000
Material handling overhead (93,000 × $4.30)	399,900
Total cost	$1,173,350
Divided by number of units	÷ 10,000
Cost per unit	$117.34

Product B

Direct material	$ 209,550
Direct labor	300,000
Utilities overhead (15,000 × $10)	150,000
Setup overhead (500 × $150)	75,000
Material handling overhead (127,000 × $4.30)	546,100
Total cost	$1,280,650
Divided by number of units	÷ 5,000
Cost per unit	$256.13

57. a.   Planning and review (P&R) = ($65,240 ÷ 93,200) = $.70 per
              billable hour   (48,000; 32,200; 12,200)
        EDP = ($72,000 ÷ 7,200) = $10 per computational hour
            (4,320; 2,400; 480)
        Personnel (Pers.) = ($56,160 ÷ 52) = $1,080 per person
            (30; 16; 6)
        Library (Libr.) = ($21,948 ÷ 186) = $118 per item
        purchased (51; 99; 36)
        Programming (Prog.) = ($56,160 ÷ 4,160) = $13.50 per
            programming hour   (1,200; 520; 2,440)
        Building (Bldg.) = ($87,000 ÷ 15,000) = $5.80 per square
            foot   (8,800; 4,875; 1,325)
        Administration (Admin.) = ($150,000 ÷ 500) = $300 per
            client   (170; 280; 50)

	A&A	Tax	Mgt. Serv.	Total
P&R	$ 34,160	$ 22,540	$ 8,540	$ 65,240
EDP	43,200	24,000	4,800	72,000
Pers.	32,400	17,280	6,480	56,160
Libr.	6,018	11,682	4,248	21,948
Prog.	16,200	7,020	32,940	56,160
Bldg.	51,040	28,275	7,685	87,000
Admin.	51,000	84,000	15,000	150,000
Total OH	$234,018	$194,797	$79,693	$508,508

b.

	A&A	Tax	Mgt. Serv.	Total
Direct costs	$1,952,000	$1,610,000	$732,000	$4,294,000
Overhead	234,018	194,797	79,693	508,508
Total cost	$2,186,018	$1,804,797	$811,693	$4,802,508

c. 1. Overhead rate = $508,508 ÷ (48,800 + 32,200 + 12,200) = $5.46 per hour

 2. A&A ($5.46 × 48,800) $266,448
     Tax ($5.46 × 32,200)   175,812
     Mgt. Serv. ($5.46 × 12,200)   66,612

d. Using the information in Part c, more cost is assigned to A&A and less to the other service areas. The consequence would be higher prices charged to A&A clients and lower prices charged to clients of the other two services than if Part b information were used.

Cases

59. a. Send/receive goods: $6,000 ÷ 500,000 = $0.012 per pound
Store goods: $4,000 ÷ 80,000 = $.05 per cubic foot
Move goods: $5,000 ÷ 5,000 = $1.00 per square foot
Identify goods: $2,000 ÷ 500 = $4 per package
Jones: (40,000 × $.012) + (3,000 × $.05) + (300 × $1) + (5 × $4) = $950
Hansen: (40,000 × $.012) + (2,000 × $.05) + (200 × $1) + (20 × $4) = $860
Assad: (40,000 × $.012) + (1,000 × $.05) + (1,000 × $1) + (80 × $4) = $1,850

b. Jones   (40,000 × $.04) $1,600
Hansen (40,000 × $.04) $1,600
Assad   (40,000 × $.04) $1,600

c. Jones   ($950 × 1.4) $1,330
Hansen ($860 × 1.4) $1,204
Assad   ($1,850 × 1.4) $2,590

d. The current pricing plan captures only one dimension of cost causality, send/receive goods. Accordingly, the prices charged for warehousing services are almost independent of the causes of the costs. As indicated in a comparison of the answers to Parts b and c, the existing pricing plan generates the same price for the three customers whereas an ABC-based price results in very different prices to be charged to the three customers.
[Adapted from Harold P. Roth and Linda T. Sims, "Costing for Warehousing and Distribution," *Management Accounting*, (August 1991) pp. 42-45.]

Chapter 5
Activity-Based Management

61. a. When product costs are calculated using ABC, the costs are assigned first to the activities causing the costs and then to the products based on the activities they consume. The following illustrates how the factory overhead costs are assigned.

Purchasing Department:

The activity driving the purchasing department costs is the number of purchase orders. With 100 purchase orders and costs of $6,000, the cost per purchase order is $60. The final assignment of costs to products is then made based on the quantity of material used in producing each product. For example, 10,000 square yards of leather were used in producing standard briefcases and 1,250 square yards were used in producing specialty briefcases. Using these quantities assigns 88.9 percent (10,000 ÷ 11,250) of the purchasing department costs for leather to standard briefcases and 11.1 percent (1,250 ÷ 11,250) to specialty briefcases. As shown in the following, similar calculations are used for the other materials.

Standard:	Leather (20 × $60 × .889)	$1,067
	Fabric (30 × $60 × .80)	1,440
	Total	$2,057
Specialty:	Leather (20 × $60 × .111)	$ 133
	Fabric (30 × $60 × .20)	360
	Synthetic (50 × $60)	3,000
	Total	$3,493

Receiving and Inspecting Materials:

The activity driving the cost of receiving and inspecting materials is the number of deliveries. The receiving and inspection cost per deliver is $50 ($7,500 ÷ 150). As with the purchasing department costs, the cost is then assigned to products based on the materials used.

Standard:	Leather (30 × $50 × .889)	$1,333
	Fabric (40 × $50 × .80)	1,600
	Total	$2,933
Specialty:	Leather (30 × $50 × .111)	$ 167
	Fabric (40 × $50 × .20)	400
	Synthetic (80 × $50)	4,000
	Total	$4,567

Setting Up Production Line:

The costs of setting up the production line are assigned to products based on the time spent performing the activity. There were 50 setups for the standard product and each requires one hour; thus, a total of 50 hours relates to standard briefcases. Similarly, the 100 setups for the specialty briefcases required two hours each for a total of 200 hours. The cost per setup hour is $40 ($10,000 ÷ 250), which results in $2,000 (50 × $40) assigned to the standard line and $8,000 (200 × $40) to the specialty line.

Inspecting Finished Goods:

The costs of inspecting the final products are assigned to the products based on the time spent on each product. The cost per hour is $20 ($8,000 ÷ 400). Thus, the total inspection cost for the standard briefcases is $3,000 (150 × $20) and for the specialty line is $5,000 (250 × $20).

Equipment-Related:

Although the equipment-related costs are caused by the process rather than a specific product, they must be allocated to determine the total costs for each product. The cost per machine hour is $.60 ($6,000 ÷ 10,000), and the cost assigned to each product is $3,000 (5,000 × $.60).

Plant-Related:

Plant-related costs are also allocated on the basis of machine hours. The cost is $1.30 ($13,000 ÷ 10,000) per machine hour, and the cost assigned to each product is $6,500 (5,000 × $1.30).

ABC Overhead Costs Summary

	Standard	Specialty
Purchasing Department	$ 2,507	$ 3,493
Receiving and Inspecting Materials	2,933	4,567
Setting Up Production Line	2,000	8,000
Inspecting Finished Goods	3,000	5,000
Equipment-Related	3,000	3,000
Plant-Related	6,500	6,500
Total	$19,940	$30,560

b.

	Standard		Specialty
DM	$20.00		$17.50
DL	6.00		3.00
OH ($19,940 ÷ 10,000)	1.99	($30,560 ÷ 2,500)	12.22
Total	$27.00		$32.72

c.   With ABC costing, the standard briefcase line now shows
      a gross profit of $2.01 ($30.00 - $27.99) per unit,
      while the specialty line shows a loss of $.72 ($32.00 -
      $32.72) per unit. Thus, CarryAll is really making a
      profit on the product that shows the loss using a
      direct labor hour basis for allocating overhead and
      losing on the specialty line that appears profitable
      using traditional allocation procedures. The president
      was correct in being concerned about the profitability
      of the products, but the problem is more with the
      specialty product line, not with the standard line.
      Traditional allocation using a volume-based measure
      results in high-volume products subsidizing low-volume
      ones, which affects the profitability of each. When
      costs are traced to products based on the activity
      causing the costs, better costing data are available
      for evaluating the profitability of the various product
      lines.

                          [Copyright 1991 IMA (formerly NAA)]

63. a.   Assignment of overhead costs:

	Columbus	Cincinnati	Dayton
General admin.	$153,839.79	$127,559.59	$127,600.62
Project costing	21,654.15	13,714.29	12,631.58
A/P; receiving	62,458.16	52,048.46	24,493.39
A/R	24,500.00	18,500.00	4,000.00
Payroll	10,298.51	11,641.79	8,059.70
Personnel recruit.	16,000.00	8,000.00	14,000.00
Employee ins.	4,805.98	5,432.83	3,761.19
Proposals	54,509.80	68,137.25	16,352.94
Sales meetings	97,104.36	74,493.53	30,402.11
Shipping	9,391.30	11,762.85	2,845.85
Ordering	19,938.46	16,246.15	11,815.38
Duplicating costs	20,000.00	18,000.00	8,000.00
Blueprinting	34,837.59	27,861.06	14,292.34
Total	$529,338.10	$453,397.80	$278,255.10
Direct overhead	180,000.00	270,000.00	177,000.00
Total overhead	$709,338.10	$723,397.80	$455,255.10

b.

	Columbus	Cincinnati	Dayton
Sales	$1,500,000	$1,419,000	$1,067,000
Direct material	(281,000)	(421,000)	(185,000)
Direct labor	(382,000)	(317,000)	(317,000)
Net contribution	$ 837,000	$ 681,000	$ 565,000

c.

	Columbus	Cincinnati	Dayton
Net contribution	$837,000.00	$681,000.00	$565,000.00
Overhead	(709,338.10)	(723,397.80)	(455,255.10)
Profit	$127,661.90	$(42,397.80)	$109,744.90

d. It is apparent that there are weaknesses in the traditional product costing system that are having a profound effect on profitability measures. Relative to profit measures based on the traditional costing measures, the ABC allocations make it apparent that the Cincinnati office is much less profitable and the Dayton office is much more profitable.

(IMA)

Ethics and Quality Discussions

65. a. In the modern competitive environment, firms must be willing to "fire" unprofitable customers so that the highest quality of service is provided to the most profitable customers. Small customers are not able to provide the same economy of operations that are available from larger customers.

b. There are ethical obligations in ending all business relationships, particularly for firms that are sole suppliers of parts or materials that are critical to their customers. At a minimum, an ethical "firing" of a customer should
   - involve an explanation as to why service is being discontinued;
   - be announced well in advance of discontinuing services to the customer;
   - be accompanied by suggestions of alternative sources of supply; and
   - be sensitive to all negative effects that will be suffered by the customer when service is ended.

c. Activity-based costing is a financial management tool. It is not a tool for ethical management of a firm, nor is it a tool that can expressly impound nonfinancial, qualitative information. To the extent that factors such as customer goodwill and market reputation are involved in decisions driven by ABC prescriptions, those factors will be ignored by activity-based management. However, it is important to acknowledge that these qualitative factors should not be ignored, and, in fact, may be important enough to overturn the activity-based prescriptions.

67.   a.   These tools help orient a firm toward managing based on
           a customer's perspective of value. World-class
           competition is based on satisfying the customer. A firm
           that accentuates activities that are highly valued by
           customers and diminishes those activities that are not
           perceived as value-added should be successful in both
           managing costs and maintaining market share.

      b.   Yes. Activity-based costing is most useful if managers
           are willing to act based on the information provided by
           the ABC system. For example, activity-based costing
           could lead to changes in product mix and product
           pricing. Top management must support the ABC
           prescriptions for the costing system to lead to
           operational improvements.

      c.   Preferably, both would be adopted. Without adopting
           ABC, the ABM prescriptions may not be understood by
           managers. But, without ABM, there may be reduced
           opportunity to identify and eliminate NVA activities.
           ABC generally requires a separate information system to
           generate activity-based information and managers might
           continue to use the firm's traditional and formal
           information systems. The two sources of information
           would inevitably give some conflicting signals and
           confuse managers. By using both ABM and ABC, actions
           taken by managers will be consistent with the
           information provided by the firm's formal information
           systems.

CHAPTER 6
COST-VOLUME-PROFIT ANALYSIS AND RELEVANT COSTING

Questions

1. The breakeven point is a point of reference by which a manager can gauge risk. The more that sales exceed the breakeven point, the smaller is the risk of not being profitable or of suffering a loss if a downturn in business occurs.

3. Breakeven analysis uses the same model as CV[P] except that the P [or profit term] is set to zero and therefore ignored.

5. The bag assumption means that a multi-product firm will consider that the products it sells are sold in a constant, proportional sales mix—as if in a bag of goods. It is necessary to make this assumption in order to determine the contribution margin for the entire company product line since individual products' contribution margins may differ significantly. Since a single contribution margin must be used in CVP analysis, the bag assumption allows CVP computations to be made.

7. The volume, profit, and selling price of a product can be expected to vary directly with the quality of the product. Cost decreases in the long run after initially increasing as quality increases.

9. In all decision-making situations, both the quantitative and qualitative factors are important. Cost-volume-profit analysis may provide useful information on a quantitative basis, but nonquantitative factors as well as long-range quantitative and qualitative items must be integrated into the process. In some instances, the qualitative factors may outweigh the quantitative.

11. For a cost to be relevant, it must be associated with the decision; it must be important to the decision maker (for example, it must be material in amount); it must differ between alternatives; and its incurrence must be in the future. If any of these factors are not true, the cost is not relevant and will not impact the firm's performance between choices of alternatives.

13. No. To be relevant, the future variable cost must also be avoidable under one or more decision options; i.e., it must vary between decision choices.

15. This statement is probably true for most businesses. However, in the long run, nearly any constraint can be overcome if there is an adequate supply of capital. To the extent capital is constrained in the long run, the capital constraint may be reflected in tight supplies of other organizational inputs including technology, managerial talent and labor.

17. Some fixed costs can be traced directly to a product line, but the discontinuation of the product line would not result in termination of the cost. Examples of such costs would include the salaries of managers who could not be dismissed if the product line were terminated, and the depreciation charges associated with production equipment for which there is no alternative use.

19. Absorption and variable costing each recognize the following as product costs: direct materials, direct labor, and variable factory overhead. Additionally, absorption costing recognizes fixed factory overhead as a product cost. Both costing approaches treat selling and administrative costs as period costs.

21. Absorption costing recognizes fixed factory overhead as a product cost. Accordingly, under absorption costing, fixed overhead flows through the inventory accounts and is eventually expensed through the cost of goods sold. Alternatively, variable costing treats fixed factory overhead as a period cost and it is deducted in its entirety in the period in which it is incurred.

23. A feasible solution is simply any solution that violates no organizational constraints. The optimal solution is also a feasible solution, but it is the one that maximizes the organizational objective function (typically maximization of profit).

Exercises

25.   a. $45,000 ÷ $9 = <u>5,000</u> units

   b. $48,000 ÷ ($8 - $5) = <u>16,000</u> units

   c. $30,000 ÷ ($12 × .25) = <u>10,000</u> units

   d.   ($48,000 ÷ .20) ÷ $12 = <u>20,000</u> units

   e. $24,000 ÷ $3 = <u>8,000</u> units; 8,000 × ($3 + $5) = <u>$64,000</u>

27.   SP is used to designate selling price.
   10,000 × (SP - .60 SP) - $40,000 = $10,000
   10,000 × (.40 SP) = $50,000
   4,000 SP = $50,000
   SP = <u>$12.50</u>

29.   a.   Units sales = ($80,000 + $40,000) ÷ $5 = <u>24,000</u> units
      24,000 × $8 = <u>$192,000</u>

   b.   Profit before taxes = $25,000 ÷ .6 = $41,667
      Unit sales = ($41,667 + $40,000) ÷ $4 = <u>20,417</u> units
      20,417 × ($6 + $4) = <u>$204,170</u>

   c.   Profit before taxes = $54,000 ÷ .6 = $90,000
      Unit sales = ($90,000 + $60,000) ÷ ($10 × .3)
                = <u>50,000</u> units
      50,000 × $10 = <u>$500,000</u>

   d.   Profit before taxes = $30,000 ÷ .50 = $60,000
      Unit sales = ($60,000 + $60,000) ÷ $3 = <u>40,000</u>
      40,000 × ($3 ÷ (1 - .7)) = <u>$400,000</u>

   e.   Profit before taxes = $40,000 ÷ .5 = $80,000
      Unit sales = ($80,000 + $25,000) ÷ (.25 × ($9 ÷ .75))
                = <u>35,000</u> units
      35,000 × ($9 ÷ .75) = <u>$420,000</u>

31. a. BEP in hours: $2,800 ÷ ($100 - $20) = \underline{35}$ hours

b. Before-tax equivalent of $8,000 after-tax:
$8,000 ÷ (1 - .20) = $10,000

Required hours = ($10,000 + $2,800) ÷ $80 = \underline{160} hours

c. Twenty-four client hours weekly will not accumulate the necessary 160 hours monthly; only 96 hours will be accumulated. Consequently, he will be 64 client hours short of achieving his profit goal.

33. a.

	Compact	Standard	Bag*
Sales	$2,000	$3,500	$9,000
Variable costs	1,800	3,000	7,800
CM	$ 200	$ 500	$1,200

*Each bag has 1 compact and 2 standard carts.

BEP = $360,000,000 ÷ $1,200 = 300,000 bags
Compact carts = 300,000 × 1 = \underline{300,000}
Standard carts = 300,000 × 2 = \underline{600,000}

b.

	Compact	Standard	Bag*
Sales	$2,000	$3,500	$5,500
Variable costs	1,800	3,000	4,800
CM	$ 200	$ 500	$ 700

*Each bag contains one compact and one standard cart.

BEP = $360,000,000 ÷ $700 = 514,286 bags (rounded)
Compact carts = 514,286 × 1 = \underline{514,286}
Standard carts = 514,286 × 1 = \underline{514,286}

In Part a, only 900,000 total carts had to be sold to break even. In Part b, a total of 1,028,572 carts must be sold to break even. The difference is caused by a shift in the sales mix requiring more of the lower (per unit) profit carts to be sold relative to the higher profit carts.

c.

	Compact	Standard	Bag*
Sales	$2,000	$3,500	$13,000
Variable costs	1,800	3,000	11,400
CM	$ 200	$ 500	$ 1,600

*Each bag contains 60% or 3 compact carts and 40% or 2 standard carts.

BEP = $425,000,000 ÷ 1,600 = 265,625 bags
Compact carts = 265,625 × 3 = 796,875
Standard carts = 265,625 × 2 = 531,250

35. a.

	Bass	**Baritone**	**Tenor**
Sales price	$15.00	$10.00	$4.00
Variable costs	14.25	9.00	3.75
CM	$ 0.75	$ 1.00	$0.25
Divide by gonganese per unit	1.25*	1.00**	0.50***
CM per pound of gonganese	$ 0.60	$ 1.00	$0.50

The firm should produce only Baritone, the product with the highest CM per pound of gonganese.

  * $6.25 ÷ $5.00 = 1.25 pounds
 ** $5.00 ÷ $5.00 = 1.00 pound
*** $2.50 ÷ $5.00 = 0.50 pound

b. Sales (30,000 units) $300,000
    Less variable costs

Gonganese	$150,000	
DL	90,000	
Variable OH	30,000	270,000
CM		$ 30,000

37. a.

Sales (100,000 × $62)	$6,200,000
Variable costs (100,000 × ($42 + $8))	5,000,000
CM	$1,200,000
Fixed costs ($500,000 + $200,000)	700,000
Projected profit	$ 500,000

b.

Sales (100,000 × 1.15 × $58)	$6,670,000
Variable costs (100,000 × 1.15 × $50)	5,750,000
CM	$ 920,000
Fixed costs	700,000
Projected profit	$ 220,000

Profit change: $500,000 - $220,000 = $280,000 decrease

c. Sales (100,000 × 1.20 × $62) $7,440,000
    Variable costs (100,000 × 1.20 × $50)   6,000,000
    CM $1,440,000
    Fixed costs ($700,000 + $200,000)   900,000
    Projected profit $ 540,000

    Profit change: $500,000 - $540,000 = $40,000 increase

39. Incremental revenue per unit $60
    Incremental manufacturing cost per unit   (40)
    Incremental selling cost per unit*   (5)
    Contribution margin $15
    Times number of units   × 32,000
    Addition to operating profit $480,000
    Current 2000 profit   80,000
    2001 operating profit $560,000

    *Note: It may be unusual for a "house" type sale to pay commission and therefore, in many cases (although not in this one), the sales commission amount would be added to the contribution margin per unit.

41. a. For product N (in thousands of dollars):
        Sales $1,400
        Variable costs   (800)
        CM $ 600
        Avoidable fixed costs and variable
          marketing costs   (525)
        Product Margin $ 75

    Product N should not be eliminated because it contributes $75,000 to the coverage of fixed costs.

    b. Elimination of product N would reduce total operating profit by $75,000 ($170,000 total operating profit before elimination of N - $95,000 total operating profit without N).

43. a. ($400,000 + $300,000 + $150,000) ÷ 100,000 = $8.50

    b. ($400,000 + $300,000 + $150,000 + $250,000) ÷ 100,000
        = $11.00

45. Normally, when we think of cost we are thinking of the collective price paid for all of the inputs to produce the product. For product costing, we have two alternatives: variable or absorption. Variable costing would provide a lower product cost than absorption costing. The company would probably prefer the absorption costing definition of cost. Such a definition would allow the company to recoup all of its product costs on sales to employees. On the other hand, the employees would probably argue that variable cost is a reasonable definition of cost. They could argue that variable cost allows the company to recoup all of the actual additional costs that it incurs because of the employee sales. In other words, the employees could argue that the fixed factory costs would be incurred whether the employees buy products or not.

47. The objective function would be to minimize total variable costs which is the sum of the individual variable costs. Or, minimize total VC, where VC = $\$.56X_1 + \$.93X_2 + \$2.12X_3 + \$1.98X_4$.

Problems

49. a.

	Laptop	Standard	Luxury	Bag
Sales	$2,200	$3,700	$6,000	$ 37,100
Variable costs	1,900	3,000	5,000	30,700
CM	$ 300	$ 700	$1,000	$ 6,400

BEP = $1,080,000,000 ÷ $6,400 = 168,750 bags
Laptop computers = 168,750 × 3 = 506,250
Standard computers = 168,750 × 5 = 843,750
Luxury computers = 168,750 × 2 = 337,500

b. Unit volume (bags)
= (($1,000,000,000 ÷ .5) + $1,080,000,000) ÷ $6,400
= 481,250 bags
Laptop computers = 481,250 × 3 = 1,443,750
Standard computers = 481,250 × 5 = 2,406,250
Luxury computers = 481,250 × 2 = 962,500

c.

	Laptop	Standard	Luxury	Bag
Sales	$2,200	$3,700	$6,000	$ 31,800
Variable costs	1,900	3,000	5,000	26,500
CM	$ 300	$ 700	$1,000	$ 5,300

Unit volume (bags)
= (($1,000,000,000 ÷ .5) + $1,080,000,000) ÷ $5,300
= 581,132 bags
Laptop computers = 581,132 × 5 = 2,905,660
Standard computers = 581,132 × 4 = 2,324,528
Luxury computers = 581,132 × 1 = 581,132

d. On a unit-for-unit basis, luxury computers generate more contribution margin than the other models. Accordingly, as the mix shifts to more luxury computers, the BEP (in units) will drop and the number of computers to be sold to reach a specified profit goal will drop.

51. a.

Total revenue per set	$24
Total variable cost per set	12
Contribution margin per set	$12
CM% for a set ($12 ÷ $24)	50%

b. BEP = $12,000 ÷ .50 = $24,000
$24,000 ÷ $24 = 1,000 sets
Hens = 1,000 × 1 = 1,000
Ducklings = 1,000 × 2 = 2,000

Hens dollar sales = 1,000 × $12 = $12,000
Ducklings dollar sales = 2,000 × $6 = 12,000
　　Total　　　　　　　　　　　　　　 $24,000

c. Revenue = ($12,000 + $24,000) ÷ .50 = $72,000
$72,000 ÷ $24 = 3,000 sets
Hens = 3,000 × 1 = 3,000
Ducklings = 3,000 × 2 = 6,000

d.
Total revenue per set	$42
Total variable cost per set	24
Contribution margin per set	$18

CM% for a set ($18 ÷ $42) = .4286

Profit before tax = $9,000 ÷ (1 - .40) = $15,000

Revenue = ($15,000 + $12,000) ÷ .4286 = $63,000
(rounded)

$63,000 ÷ $42 = 1,500 sets
Hens = 1,500 × 1 = 1,500
Ducklings = 1,500 × 5 = 7,500

53. a. The rationing decision should be based on a comparison of the contribution margin that can be generated from each product per unit (minute, hour, or day) of oven time:

	Birthday Cakes	Wedding Cakes	Sp. Occasion Cakes
Sales	$ 25	$100	$ 40
Variable Costs			
Direct materials	5	30	10
Direct labor	5	15	8
Variable overhead	2	5	4
Variable selling	3	12	5
Contribution Margin	$ 10	$ 38	$ 13
Required oven time	10 min.	80 min.	18 min.
Contribution margin per minute of oven time	$1	$0.475	$0.722

Since the birthday cakes generate the highest contribution margin per minute of oven time, and given the fact that demand for birthday cakes is high enough to consume all of the oven's available time, only birthday cakes should be produced. This use of the oven will maximize company profit.

b.   Total available oven time in minutes = 690 × 60 =
     41,400. According to the conclusion in Part a, only
     birthday cakes will be produced:
     Production in units: 41,400 ÷ 10 = 4,140 birthday
             cakes

Sales (4,140 × $25)	$103,500
Variable costs:	
Direct materials (4,140 × $5)	20,700
Direct labor (4,140 × $5)	20,700
Variable overhead (4,140 × $2)	8,280
Variable selling (4,140 × $3)	12,420
Total variable costs	$ 62,100
Contribution margin	$ 41,400
Fixed costs:	
Factory	(1,200)
Selling & Administrative	(800)
Operating income	$ 39,400

c.   The marketing manager needs to be sensitive to how the
     seasons affect the demand for the company's products.
     For example, since demand is much higher during the
     holiday season, the marketing manager needs to be
     focused on selling the mix of products that will
     maximize the firm's contribution margin.
          Alternatively, during other seasons when demand is
     slack, the marketing manager simply needs to
     concentrate on promoting all products; capacity
     constraints will not be a consideration. Since
     virtually all fixed costs are irrelevant in the short
     term, the marketing manager should be willing to accept
     all orders that generate a positive contribution
     margin.

55. a.   Opportunity cost occurs because Mary Ann loses the
          contribution margin on each of the 2,000 units of sales
          she would surrender to accept the English order:
          Opportunity cost = selling price - all variable
          expenses
                 = $50 - ($6.00 + $6.50 + $10.00 + $3.00) = $24.50

b.   Direct materials ($6.00 + $.50) $ 6.50
       Direct labor   6.50
       Variable overhead   10.00
       Fixed overhead   12.00
       Variable selling expenses   0.00
       Opportunity cost (from (a) above less fixed OH
       included)   12.50
       Total costs $47.50
       Required extra amount to accept offer   1.00
       Minimum price $48.50

c.   Added operating profit should be $1 × 2,000 stuffed
       animals = $2,000

d.

Without New Offer   **With New Offer**

Sales (20,000 × $50) $1,000,000   Sales (18,000 × $50) +
                                           (2,000 × $48.50) $997,000

Expenses   Expenses
                                           (18,000 × $37.50)
   (20,000 × $37.50)   750,000   + [2,000 × ($6.50
                                          + $6.50 + $10.00
                                          + $12.00)]   745,000
Operating Profit $ 250,000   Operating Profit $252,000

       Added operating profit = $252,000 - $250,000 = $2,000

57. a.

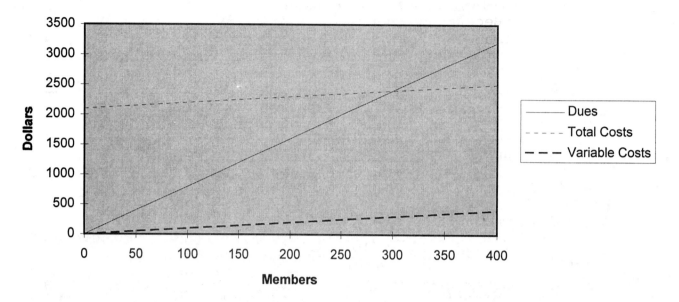

b.

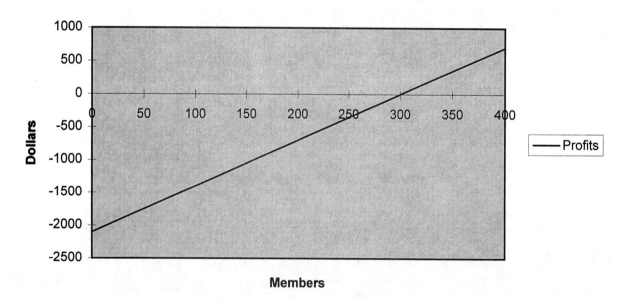

c. The breakeven chart is more appropriate because the Senior Citizens Club, as a not-for-profit organization, is expected to break even but not earn a profit.

59.   a.   CM = $150 - $40 = $110 or 73.33%
            BEP = FC ÷ CM = $1,800,000 ÷ $110
                  = 16,364 passengers (rounded)
            BEP = FC ÷ CM% = $1,800,000 ÷.7333
                  = $2,454,657 revenues*
            *Because of rounding, a slightly different answer is
            found as follows: 16,364 passengers × $150
                  = $2,454,600 revenue

      b.   120 × .70 = 84 seats per plane filled
            16,364 ÷ 84 = 195 flights (rounded)

      c.   CM = $200 - $40 = $160
            120 × .55 = 66 filled seats
            BEP = FC ÷ CM = $1,800,000 ÷ $160 = 11,250 passengers
            11,250 ÷ 66 = 171 flights (rounded)

      d.   CM = $150 - $60 = $90
            BEP = FC ÷ CM = $1,800,000 ÷ $90 = 20,000 passengers
            20,000 ÷ 84 = 239 flights (rounded)

      e.   After tax profit = $600,000 ÷ (1 - tax rate)
            = $600,000 ÷ (1 - .4) = $600,000 ÷ .6 = $1,000,000
            $180X = $2,000,000 + $50X + $1,000,000
            $130X = $3,000,000
            X = 23,077 passengers

      f.   CM for discounted fares = $120 - $40 = $80 × 12
            discounted seats = $960 each flight × 40 flights per
            day × 30 days per month = $1,152,000;
            $1,152,000 minus $100,000 additional fixed costs =
            $1,052,000 additional coverage toward pretax profits
            each month.

g.   (1)   New CM = $175 - $40 = $135; 120 × .60 = 72 seats;
72 × $135 × 20 = new CM of $194,400, compared to
$100,000 additional fixed costs. Therefore, the
company should obtain the route.

(2) $175X = $100,000 + $40X + $57,500
$135X = $157,500
X = 1,167 passengers
1,167 ÷ 72 = 17 flights per month (rounded)

(3)   120 × .75 = 90 seats filled
1,167 ÷ 90 = 13 flights (rounded)

(4)   Southern States should consider such things as:

■   connections to other Southern States flights
that might be made by these passengers,

■   long-range potential for increased load
factors,

■   increased customer goodwill in this new
market,

■   increased employment opportunities for labor
in the area, and

■   competition in the market.

Ethics and Quality Discussions

61. a. For a large automaker, setting the sales mix so that breakeven analysis could be conducted would be relatively difficult. Consideration of the impact of changes to the sales mix further compounds this difficulty. Another difficulty would be distinguishing between variable and fixed costs. Some costs are difficult to classify. Another problem is that in the real world neither revenue nor costs are likely to be strictly a linear function of sales volume. Accordingly, knowledge of assumptions about the nature of nonlinearities in the cost and revenue structures would be required. Another variable would be where units would be sold. Domestic sales relative to international sales may have entirely different consequences for costs and revenues. Further, the president would be required to make assumptions about short-term pricing behavior; this may be extraordinarily difficult because it might require knowledge of competitors' actions. Much short-term pricing may simply be reactive based on actions of other automakers.

  Another point is that the president may think of breakeven as more of a long-run concept that relates more to individual product lines (rather than the entire company at a specific point in time) in a life-cycle concept. This would be logical because of the huge up-front costs associated with launching a new vehicle.

  b. The congressional investigator may have been basing his statement on the fact that knowing the breakeven point is crucial management information. Because this president indicated he had no exact notion about the breakeven point, the congressional investigator may have concluded that the president was an ineffective manager. However, it is likely that the investigator possesses little knowledge about the complexity of the automotive industry. If he understood some of the complicating factors mentioned in Part a, he would likely have a different opinion of the president.

63. a. There is nothing illegal about Klein pushing a certain kind of product.

    b. Klein is responding to incentives created by the company. In designing the commission plan, management has totally ignored the relative profitability of its various products. By establishing an incentive scheme based on a straight percentage of sales, it is encouraging the sales people to sell the highest priced products.

    c. Management would probably take the view that every employee has a responsibility to consider the impact of their actions on corporate profitability. By pushing only high-priced items, Klein is making the company less profitable than it would be if a mix of products were sold. Management would probably suggest that Klein has an obligation to consider the relative profitability of each product as well as the affect of each sale on his personal compensation.

    d. Klein should take the information about relative profitability to management. He should show them how they have created incentives for him to sell only high-priced items which are less profitable than the low-priced items. He should suggest that a new compensation program be created, perhaps based on product contribution margin rather than product sales. This would automatically provide Klein an incentive to sell products that generated the most corporate profit per unit of effort.

CHAPTER 7
THE BUDGET PROCESS

Questions

1. Budgeting has significant advantages in improving
    communications, motivation, coordination and teamwork. It
    allows management to visualize the future state of affairs in
    time to make adjustments in order to effect more desirable
    results. It is a major tool in planning and controlling. The
    more complex and diversified the company, and the greater the
    degree of competitive intensity it faces, the more important
    budgeting is.

3. Most organizations use participatory budgeting for the
    following reasons: because inputs and judgments from all
    levels of the organization can be considered, because the
    budget becomes a more intimate part of the working lives of
    operating personnel since they had a say in its development,
    and because it is a more effective means of engendering a
    spirit of coordinated teamwork in accomplishing goals and
    objectives. Disadvantages are that the approach is more time
    consuming and that dysfunctional behavior on the part of
    either top managers (e.g., making undiscussed major changes)
    or subordinates (e.g., empire building and including budgetary
    slack) can undermine the process.

5. | **Sections of budget manual** | | **Reasons for the section** |
    |---|---|---|
    | a. | Statement of purposes & desired results | a. To communicate as a first step of coordination |
    | b. | Budgetary activities to be performed | b. To designate who and what is responsible |
    | c. | Calendar of budgetary activities | c. To indicate timetable and provide coordination of efforts |
    | d. | Sample forms preparation | d. To provide for consistency |
    | e. | Original, revised & approved budgets | e. To reflect revision of process and to serve as a control document |

Chapter 7
The Budget Process

7. The diversity of resources used, activities conducted, and quantities of funds provided/used generally make budgeting more important to a business than to an individual. In addition, there is no assurance of the continuity of management and, therefore, written plans are more useful than spoken plans (which may work to manage personal and family finances). The real value in writing down plans is that psychologically it is the first step to commitment to those plans.

9. It is said to be a static budget because it is based on a single level of demand. It must be static to facilitate the many time-consuming financial arrangements that must be made before beginning operations for the budget year.

11. The master budget is driven entirely by expected sales. Without sales, the firm would have no need to acquire resources or remain in operation. This, of course, assumes that the firm does not have demand in excess of its production capacity. In that case, capacity becomes the budget driver.

13. The materials purchases budget is driven by the production budget and the firm's inventory policies with respect to materials. Since materials are required for production to commence, the amount of materials acquired in a particular period will reflect the production budget for that period. However, the material purchases budget will not be strictly proportional to production if the firm desires to increase or decrease its level of materials inventory.

15. Overhead must be separated into variable and fixed components so that it can be estimated. By separating overhead costs into variable and fixed cost pools, the volume dependent costs (variable) can be estimated as a function of production volume specified in the production budget, and the fixed costs can be estimated as a lump sum equal to the total of the individual costs that comprise the fixed overhead cost pool.

17. Managers must control cash in order to be able to pay the company's obligations when due. The cash budget is essential in control of cash in terms of: (1) cash available exclusive of financing, (2) cash excess/inadequacy, (3) cash available/needed, and (4) financing options for acquisition of needed cash or disposition of unneeded cash.

19. A firm's credit policies significantly affect the cash collection pattern. Liberal credit terms allow customers to pay at some point in the future without incurring substantial interest costs. Alternatively, a tight credit policy is designed to encourage credit-sale customers to pay early. The cash collection pattern is further influenced by policies regarding which customers should be granted credit. If risky customers are granted too much credit, uncollectible accounts will rise. If less risky customers are denied credit, total sales and cash collections will decline.

   A firm gives a discount for cash sales to encourage customers to pay cash for purchases rather than buy on credit. The customer can equate the cash discount to an interest expense incurred on credit purchases.

21. Pro forma financial statements allow management to view the results of their plans for the period and decide whether those results are acceptable. If the results are unacceptable, management still has time to change or adjust items before the start of the period. This might mean increasing or decreasing prices or costs or revising their expectations about objectives and goals.

23. When the projected cash balance on the pro forma balance sheet is compared with the beginning of the budget year cash balance, the expected change in cash for the budget year can be calculated. The statement of cash flows explains how this expected change in cash is related to the firm's operating, investing and financing activities.

25. The spreadsheet program allows managers to do "what if" analyses. This type of analysis allows the management team to evaluate the effects of errors in their estimates or possible changes in the plans. By linking the various budgets in the spreadsheet, a change can be made in one variable and its effects will automatically flow through all affected budgets. For example, the sales estimates could be changed and the impact of the sales change on all budgets would be shown immediately.

27. The sales price variance measures the difference between actual and budgeted total revenues that is attributable to a difference in unit sales price. The sales volume variance captures the difference between actual and total budgeted sales that is attributable to a difference in unit volume. Together, the two variances explain the difference between total actual revenues and total budgeted revenues.

Chapter 7
The Budget Process

Exercises

29. a. 5
    b. 6
    c. 7
    d. 3
    e. 4
    f. 2
    g. 1
    h. 9
    i. 8

31.

		July	August	September	Total
	Sales	8,000	10,000	11,000	29,000
+	Desired end. balance	800	880	960	960
=	Total needed	8,800	10,880	11,960	29,960
−	Beginning balance	640*	800	880	640
=	Production	8,160	10,080	11,080	29,320

*(.08 × 8,000)

33.

		Flipper Production
	Sales	15,200
+	Desired ending balance	7,200
=	Total needed	22,400
−	Beginning balance	3,300
=	Production - pairs	19,100

		Lbs. Rubber Purchases
	Production (2 × 19,100)	38,200
+	Desired ending balance	16,000
=	Total needed	54,200
−	Beginning balance	10,200
=	Purchases	44,000 pounds

35. a. $y = \$320,000 + (\$14.25 \times 12,000) = \underline{\$491,000}$

    b. Cash spent = $491,000 - $35,000 = $456,000

37. a. $194,000 - $140,000 = $54,000 portion remaining of April billings
    $54,000 ÷ .3 = $180,000 April billings

    b. $140,000 ÷ .70 = $200,000 May billings
    .01 × 200,000 = $2,000 uncollectible from May billings

    c. Collections in June:
    .29 of April billings of $180,000 = $ 52,200
    .40 of May billings of $200,000 = 80,000
    .30 of June billings of $210,000 = 63,000
    Total June collections $195,200

d.   The oral report should contain at least two methods of manipulating credit sales. Credit sales could be collected sooner if management would tighten credit policies. One method of tightening the credit policy is to simply allow fewer customers to have credit privileges. Another less onerous possibility is to provide a larger discount for cash sales. This is a method that provides customers more incentive to pay early. The credit-paying times can also be shortened.

e.   The two important variables would be the effect the change in credit sales would have on sales and the effect the change would have on cash collections and delinquent and bad accounts. The analysis should treat as a benefit the savings in interest costs from earlier cash collections and fewer bad debts. The analysis should treat as a cost the contribution margin of lost sales resulting from the change in credit policy.

39. a.

	Units to be purchased	68,300
×	Cost per unit	× 3.80
=	Cost of purchases	$259,540
×	% payment for current month	× .40
=	Increase in accounts payable	$103,816
-	Discounts ($103,816 × .5 × .02)	(1,038)
=	Cash payments for current month	$102,778
+	Payment for October	207,936[1]
	Cash payments for accounts payable	$310,714

[1] 91,200 × $3.80 × .60

b.   Managers could ask creditors for additional time to pay accounts. The other typical alternatives to raise short-term cash are to borrow from a commercial lender or to sell assets (e.g., factor receivables).

41.

Abbott Supplies

Pro Forma Cost of Goods Manufactured Schedule

For the Period Ending December 31, 1999

Work in process–January 1		$ 9,200
Cost of direct materials used:		
Direct materials balance–Jan. 1	$ 2,300	
Purchases of direct materials	287,700	
Total available	$290,000	
Direct materials balance–Dec. 31	5,200	
Cost of direct materials used	$284,800	
Direct labor	106,700	
Factory overhead	115,500	507,000
Total costs to be accounted for		$516,200
Work in process–Dec. 31		3,300
Cost of goods manufactured		$512,900

43.

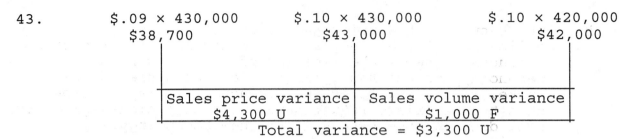

          $.09 × 430,000 $.10 × 430,000 $.10 × 420,000
              $38,700 $43,000 $42,000

                    | Sales price variance | Sales volume variance |
                    | $4,300 U | $1,000 F |
                          Total variance = $3,300 U

The dairy sold 10,000 gallons more than budget and this
generated $1,000 of additional revenue. However, the dairy
sold its output at $.01 per gallon below the expected selling
price and this lost $4,300 of expected revenues. These two
factors are combined to explain the $3,300 revenue shortfall.

Problems
45.   Production

	January	February	March	Total
Sales	36,000	32,000	30,000	98,000
Desired ending balance	8,000	7,500	7,000	7,000
Total needed	44,000	39,500	37,000	105,000
Estimated beg. balance	9,000	8,000	7,500	9,000
Production	35,000	31,500	29,500	96,000

Purchases—Direct material M

	January	February	March	Total
Production (times 3)	105,000	94,500	88,500	288,000
Desired ending balance	6,000	5,625	5,250	5,250
Total needed	111,000	100,125	93,750	293,250
Estimated beg. balance	6,750	6,000	5,625	6,750
Purchases in pounds	104,250	94,125	88,125	286,500

Purchases—Direct material N

	January	February	March	Total
Production (times 2)	70,000	63,000	59,000	192,000
Desired ending balance	4,000	3,750	3,500	3,500
Total needed	74,000	66,750	62,500	195,500
Estimated beg. balance	4,500	4,000	3,750	4,500
Purchases in pounds	69,500	62,750	58,750	191,000

Purchases—Direct material O

	January	February	March	Total
Production (times 4)	140,000	126,000	118,000	384,000
Desired ending balance	8,000	7,500	7,000	7,000
Total needed	148,000	133,500	125,000	391,000
Estimated beg. balance	9,000	8,000	7,500	9,000
Purchases in pounds	139,000	125,500	117,500	382,000

b. The nature of the production process affects the efficiency of the conversion of materials into finished products. One of the benefits of utilizing higher technology is the reduction that can be achieved in waste, scrap, and defective products. It may be expected that the materials required per unit of finished products will drop to some extent if the new technology is acquired.

c. The vendor of the new technology, an in-house engineering department, and knowledgeable production managers should be able to offer valuable insights as to how material requirements will change with acquisition of the machine technology. In fact, the change in material requirements is likely to have been one of the factors that was considered in evaluating the purchase of the new technology.

47. a. **Production Budget**

Sales	200,000
Desired ending finished goods	12,000 (1)
Total needed	212,000
Beginning finished goods (given)	5,000
Production	207,000

(1) 240,000 one pound bags of coffee × .05

Purchases of bags:

Production	207,000
Desired ending balance	12,000
Total needed	219,000
Beginning inventory	12,000
Purchases of bags	207,000

b. **Purchases of coffee beans:**

Production (207,000 × 15/16)	194,062.50
Desired ending balance (12,000 × 15/16)	11,250.00
Total needed	205,312.50
Beginning inventory	14,000.00
Purchases of pounds of coffee beans	191,312.50

c. **Purchases of additional ingredients**

Production (207,000 × 1/16)	12,937.50
Desired ending balance (12,000 × 1/16)	750.00
Total needed	13,687.50
Beginning inventory	1,100.00
Purchases of pounds of add. ingredients	12,587.50

d.

Purchase of bags (207,000 × $.14)	$ 28,980.00
Purchase of coffee beans (191,312.50 × $1.52)	290,795.00
Purchase of additional ingredients	
(12,587.50 × $.20)	2,517.50
Total dollars of purchases	$322,292.50

e. $322,292.50 × .60 × (1 - .02) = $189,508 (rounded)

f.   JIT would allow the firm to gradually reduce its
      inventories of finished goods, work in process, and raw
      materials. This would result in substantial cost savings
      and new insights into improving existing operations.

49.   a.   **Production Budget:**

	Jan.	Feb.	March	Total	April
Sales	6,400	5,200	7,400	19,000	8,000
Desired ending balance	1,040	1,480	1,600	1,600	1,600
Total needed	7,440	6,680	9,000	20,600	9,600
Estimated beg. balance	4,220	1,040	1,480	4,220	1,600
Production	3,220	5,640	7,520	16,380	8,000

b.   **Purchases Budget**

Scrap Iron (in pounds)	Jan.	Feb.	Mar.	Total
Production (times 2)	6,440	11,280	15,040	32,760
Desired ending balance	2,820	3,760	4,000	4,000
Total needed	9,260	15,040	19,040	36,760
Beginning balance	2,000	2,820	3,760	2,000
Unit purchases (lbs.)	7,260	12,220	15,280	34,760
Unit price × units	$14,520	$24,440	$30,560	$69,520

Bookstand Bases (units)	Jan.	Feb.	Mar.	Total
Production	3,220	5,640	7,520	16,380
Desired ending balance	1,410	1,880	2,000	2,000
Total needed	4,630	7,520	9,520	18,380
Beginning balance	3,200	1,410	1,880	3,200
Unit purchases	1,430	6,110	7,640	15,180
Unit price × units	$2,574	$10,998	$13,752	$27,324
Total purchases	$17,094	$35,438	$44,312	$96,844

c.

Cash payments from:	January	February	March	Total
Dec. Accounts Payable	$ 5,800.00			$ 5,800.00
Jan.(17,094 ×.75 ×.99)	12,692.30			12,692.30
Jan.(17,094 ×.25)		$ 4,273.50		4,273.50
Feb.(35,438 ×.75 ×.99)		26,312.72		26,312.72
Feb.(35,438 ×.25)			$ 8,859.50	8,859.50
Mar.(44,312 ×.75 ×.99)			32,901.66	32,901.66
Total	$18,492.30	$30,586.22	$41,761.16	$90,839.68

d. **Cash payments for factory overhead and period expenses:**

	January	February	March	Total
Factory overhead:				
$24,000 + $1.30X	$28,186	$31,332	$33,776	$ 93,294
(where X = production)				
Period expenses:				
$13,600 + $.10X	20,960	19,580	22,110	62,650
(where X = sales)				
Total	$49,146	$50,912	$55,886	$155,944

e.
Iberville Furniture Co.
Pro Forma Cash Budget
For Three Months and First Quarter of 1999

	January	February	March	Total
Beg. cash balance	$18,320.00	$24,627.70	$ 15,481.48	$ 18,320.00
Cash collections	76,200.00	61,300.00	81,100.00	218,600.00
Total available exclusive of financing	$94,520.00	$85,927.70	$ 96,581.48	$236,920.00
Disbursements:				
Cash payments for purchases	$18,492.30	$30,586.22	$ 41,761.16	$ 90,839.68
Direct labor [1]	2,254.00	3,948.00	5,264.00	11,466.00
Cash payments-OH & period expenses	49,146.00	50,912.00	55,886.00	155,944.00
Total disbursements	$69,892.30	$85,446.22	$102,911.16	$258,249.68
Cash excess or (inadequacy)	$24,627.70	$ 481.48	$ (6,329.68)	$(21,329.68)
Minimum cash balance desired	15,000.00	15,000.00	15,000.00	15,000.00
Cash available or (needed)	$ 9,627.70	($14,518.52)	$(21,329.68)	$(36,329.68)
Financing:				
Borrowings (repayment)	0.00	15,000.00	22,000.00	37,000.00
Interest (paid)	0.00			
Total effect of financing	0.00	$15,000.00	$ 22,000.00	$ 37,000.00
Ending cash balance	$24,627.70	$15,481.48	$ 15,670.32	$ 15,670.32

[1] Units of production × $.70

f. An inside source of information would be the purchasing department. The purchasing department would have information on credit terms for all major suppliers. The accounting clerk could confirm the credit policy by calling the vendors directly.

51. a.

Collections In/From	January	February	March
January			
Oct. $122,000 × .9 × .1	$ 10,980.00		
Nov. 128,000 × .9 × .4	46,080.00		
Dec. 133,000 × .9 × .1 × .99	11,850.30		
Dec. 133,000 × .9 × .4	47,880.00		
Jan. 141,000 × .1 × .99	13,959.00		
February			
Nov. 128,000 × .9 × .1		$ 11,520.00	
Dec. 133,000 × .9 × .4		47,880.00	
Jan. 141,000 × .9 × .1 × .99		12,563.10	
Jan. 141,000 × .9 × .4		50,760.00	
Feb. 139,000 × .1 × .99		13,761.00	
March			
Dec. 133,000 × .9 × .1			$ 11,970.00
Jan. 141,000 × .9 × .4			50,760.00
Feb. 139,000 × .9 × .1 × .99			12,384.90
Feb. 139,000 × .9 × .4			50,040.00
Mar. 124,000 × .1 × .99			12,276.00
Totals	$130,749.30	$136,484.10	$137,430.90

b.

Purchases	January	February	March	Total
Estimated sale (at cost)	$ 70,500	$ 69,500	$ 62,000	$202,000
+ Desired end inv. (75%)	52,125	46,500	47,625[1]	47,625[2]
Total needs	$122,625	$116,000	$109,625	$249,625
- Beginning inventory	52,875	52,125	46,500	52,875
= Budgeted purchases	$ 69,750	$ 63,875	$ 63,125	$196,750

[1],[2] (127,000 ÷ 2) × .75 (i.e., one-half April sales × .75)

c.

Cash Payments for Purchases	January	February	March
In January/From			
December	$ 41,700		
January ($69,750 × .4)	27,900		
In February/From			
January ($69,750 × .6)		$ 41,850	
February ($63,875 × .4)		25,550	
In March/From			
February ($63,875 × .6)			$ 38,325
March ($63,125 × .4)			25,250

Cash payments for S & A:

Sales			
Dec. 133,000	7,120[1]		
Jan. 141,000	11,160[2]	7,440[3]	
Feb. 139,000		11,040[4]	7,360[5]
Mar. 124,000			10,140[6]
Total monthly disbursements	$87,880	$85,880	$81,075

(1) .4 [(.1 × $133,000) + $6,000 - $1,500]
(2) .6 [(.1 × $141,000) + $6,000 - $1,500]
(3) .4 [(.1 × $141,000) + $6,000 - $1,500]
(4) .6 [(.1 × $139,000) + $6,000 - $1,500]
(5) .4 [(.1 × $139,000) + $6,000 - $1,500]
(6) .6 [(.1 × $124,000) + $6,000 - $1,500]

53.   a.   **Lawrence Rubber Co.**
                            Pro forma Income Statement
                              For February, 1999

Sales	$220,000
Cost of Goods Sold	165,000
Gross Margin	$ 55,000
Other expenses	(41,000)
Net income before taxes	$ 14,000

      b.   **Lawrence Rubber Co.**
                            Pro forma Balanced Sheet
                              February 28, 1999

Cash	$ 28,000 [1]
Accounts receivable	83,600 [2]
Inventory	47,000 [3]
Property, plant & equipment (net)	60,000
Total assets	$218,600
Accounts payable	$180,000
Common stock	100,000
Retained earnings	(61,400)
Total liabilities and owners' equity	$218,600

[1] Beginning cash balance $ 16,000
    Collections from prior months' sales   76,000
    Collections from current sales   132,000
    Less payments on account   (196,000)
    Ending cash balance $ 28,000
[2] (.4 × $220,000) - (.02 × $220,000)
[3] $32,000 + (.75 × $240,000) - (.75 × $220,000)

c. This company has a negative net retained earnings. Accordingly, it will be very difficult for the company to borrow funds needed for operating. If it can obtain financing, it will be required to pay extraordinary rates of interest and pledge specific assets for collateral. One thing the company could do is sell the accounts receivable. The cash acquired could be used to finance operations and reduce accounts payable. The firm should also examine its assets. If there are assets that have market values significantly above book values, the assets could be sold to increase income, reduce the negative retained earnings, and increase cash. However, the company must be very careful to avoid selling assets that are critical to its ability to remain a going concern. Additionally, the company should try to reduce the level of inventory; this will generate cash, increase income, and reduce the deficit in retained earnings.

55. a.

	Product A	Product B
Budgeted sales	$96,000	$48,000
Budgeted CGS	48,000	32,000
Budgeted GM	$48,000	$16,000

b.

	Product A	Product B
Actual sales	$85,000	$75,000
Actual CGS	50,000	60,000
Actual GM	$35,000	$15,000

c.

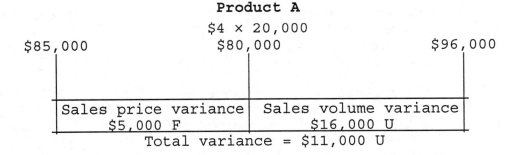

Product A

$4 × 20,000

| $85,000 | $80,000 | $96,000 |

| Sales price variance | Sales volume variance |
| $5,000 F | $16,000 U |

Total variance = $11,000 U

Product B

$3 × 30,000

| $75,000 | $90,000 | $48,000 |

| Sales price variance | Sales volume variance |
| $15,000 U | $42,000 F |

Total variance = $27,000 F

d. The reason is that an analysis of the difference between budgeted and actual gross margin requires an analysis of differences between actual and budgeted product costs as well as actual and budgeted revenues.

57.   a.   Compute actual sales volume:
           Daniel Boone: $391,000 ÷ $230 = 1,700 units
           Easter Bunny: $282,800 ÷ $140 = 2,020 units
           Pocahontas: $622,500 ÷ $150 = 4,150 units

           Sales price variances:
           Daniel Boone: 1,700 × ($240 - $230) = $17,000 U
           Easter Bunny: 2,020 × ($130 - $140) = 20,200 F
           Pocahontas: 4,150 × ($160 - $150) =   41,500 U
              Total $38,300 U

      b.   Daniel Boone: $240 × (1,600 - 1,700) = $24,000 F
           Easter Bunny: $130 ×(2,150 - 2,020) = 16,900 U
           Pocahontas: $160 × (4,200 - 4,150) =   8,000 U
              Total $ 900 U

      c.   Overall, the revenue variance was $38,300 + $900 =
           $39,200. Most of this unfavorable result was caused by
           the price variances which were negative on both Daniel
           Boone and Pocahontas sales. These results could be
           attributed to short-term economic pressures, or marketing
           tactics employed by Mr. Navarez. Assuming the results
           reflect a rational strategy, Mr. Navarez may have
           accepted lower prices and overall lower volume to save
           costs. For example, he may have reduced advertising and
           promotion or reduced the commissions paid to sales
           people. It is therefore possible that actual net income
           was above the budgeted level.

      d.   As indicated in Part b, the overall sales variance is
           $39,200 unfavorable, or below budget. The biggest
           negative deviations from budget are associated with the
           sales prices for Daniel Boones and Pocahontases, as well
           as reduced volume for Easter Bunnies. A partial offset
           to these negative deviations resulted from a positive
           sales price variance for Easter Bunnies and a positive
           volume variance for Daniel Boones. Overall, both Easter
           Bunnies and Daniel Boones showed favorable deviations
           from budget, the Pocahontases had both unfavorable price
           and volume variances.

Chapter 7
The Budget Process

Cases

59. a.

The Mason Agency
Revised Operating Budget
Fourth Quarter 1999-2000

Revenues		
Consulting fees		
Management consulting		$468,000
EDP consulting		478,125
Total consulting revenue		$946,125
Other revenue		10,000
Total revenue		$956,125
Expenses		
Consulting salary expense	$510,650	
Travel and related expense	57,875	
General and administrative expense	93,000	
Depreciation expense	40,000	
Corporate allocation	75,000	
Total expenses		776,525
Operating income		$179,600

Supporting computations:

Schedule of projected revenues for fourth quarter 1999-2000

	Mgmt. Consulting		EDP Consulting	
Third Quarter				
Revenues		$315,000		$ 421,875
Divided by billing rate	÷	$90	÷	$75
Billable hours	=	3,500	=	5,625
Divided by # of consultants	÷	10	÷	15
Hours per consultant	=	350	=	375
Fourth quarter				
Planned increase		50		50
Billable hours per consultant		400		425
Multiplied by # of consultants	×	13	×	15
Billable hours	=	5,200	=	6,375
Multiplied by billing rate	×	$90	×	$75
Projected revenue	=	$468,000	=	$478,125

Schedules of projected salaries, travel, general and administrative, and allocated corporate expenses

	Mgmt. Consulting	EDP Consulting
Compensation		
Existing consultants		
Annual salary	$ 50,000	
($50,000 × 92%)		$ 46,000
Quarterly salary	$ 12,500	$ 11,500
Planned increase (10%)	1,250	1,150
Total	$ 13,750	$ 12,650
Multiplied by #		
of consultants	10	15
Total	$137,500	$189,750
New consultants (3) at old		
salary (3 × $12,500)	37,500	0
Total	$175,000	$189,750
Benefits (40%)	70,000	75,900
Total	$245,000	$265,650

Total compensation = $245,000 + $265,650 = $510,650

Travel expense

Management consultants (400 hrs. × 13)		5,200
EDP consultants (425 hrs. × 15)		6,375
Total hours		11,575
Rate per hour*		× $5
Total travel expense		$57,875

    *Third quarter travel expense divided by hours = rate per hour ($45,625 ÷ 9,125 = $5)

General and administrative ($100,000 × 93%) $93,000

Corporate allocation ($50,000 × 150%) $75,000

b.   An organization would prepare a revised forecast when the assumptions underlying the original forecast are no longer valid. The assumptions may involve factors outside or inside the company. Changes in assumptions involving external factors may include changes in demand for the company's products or services, changes in the cost of various inputs to the company, or changes in the economic or political environment in which the company operates. Changes in assumptions involving internal factors may include changes in company goals or objectives by management or stockholders.

(CMA adapted)

61.   a. and b.

                              CME, INC.
                            Cash Budgets
                           (000s omitted)

	For the year ending December 31, 1999	For month ending January 31, 1999
Cash balance, Jan. 1	$ 750	$ 750
Cash receipts:		
Program revenue	12,000	1,440[3]
Membership income	10,000[1]	0
Total cash available	$22,750	$2,190
Cash outflows:		
Seminar:		
Instruction fees	$ 8,400[2]	$ 0
Facilities	5,600	672[4]
Promotion	1,000	100[5]
Total	$15,000	$772
Salaries	960	80[6]
Benefits, staff	240	18[7]
Office lease	240	20[8]
Gen. admin.	1,500	125
Gen. promotion	600	50[9]
Research grants	3,000	500
Cap. expenditures	510	102[10]
Total	22,050	1,667
Ending cash balance	$ 700	$ 523

Supporting calculations:

[1]   100,000 members × $100 = $10,000,000

[2] $12,000,000 × 70% = $8,400,000

[3] $12,000,000 × 12% = $1,440,000

[4] $5,600,000 × 12% = $672,000

[5] $1,000,000 ÷ 10 = $100,000 (no seminar promotion in June
        & July)

[6] $960,000 ÷ 12 = $80,000

[7]   ($240,000 - $24,000) ÷ 12 = $18,000

[8] $240,000 ÷ 12 = $20,000

[9] $600,000 ÷ 12 = $50,000

[10] $510,000 ÷ 5 = $102,000

c.   The most important operating problem faced by CME, Inc. is the
       short-term liquidity. During the first six months, expenditures
       of $14.5 million are forecasted to be slightly more than double
       the revenue ($7.2 million). This will necessitate short-term
       borrowing during the second and third quarters of the year. The
       second most important problem is that the cash expenditures are
       forecasted to exceed revenue by $50,000 and this could be
       further compounded by interest on short-term borrowing which
       apparently has not been forecasted. The fees do not fully
       support the seminars. The total of the facility costs and the
       faculty costs exceed the seminar revenues.

                                              (CMA adapted)

Ethics and Quality Discussion

63. a. This is an interesting question, and there seems to be substantial disagreement on the answer. Some argue that customers are those that hire the graduates of the university. Some argue that students are the customers; still others argue that society is the customer. Students are likely to have interesting views and comments on this question.

   b. Many students will agree that their accounting department offers a curriculum that is heavily oriented to financial accounting and auditing; some will disagree. The issue provides an interesting topic to be debated.

   c. It is argued that public accounting represents a very well-defined market for accounting graduates. The job requirements, perhaps as defined by the criteria to become a CPA, are easy to identify and therefore an appropriate curriculum can be devised easily. Alternatively, the skills needed to practice accounting in industry are likely to vary substantially from job to job and company to company.

   A further consideration is that public accounting is organized to provide feedback to colleges and universities regarding their performance. Additionally, public accounting firms, particularly the Big Six, provide substantial sums of money to large accounting departments to support research and teaching development. This substantial support may be a source of bias in course offerings.

   d. Like all service providers, colleges and universities need to be sensitive to the needs of their customers. Placing yourself in the role of customer, you have the right to provide feedback to the accounting department regarding the extent to which you feel its courses meet your needs as a consumer. Also, there are obvious ways to bring political pressure to bear in the interest of change through state legislatures or alumni associations.

65. a. In an unusual situation, where the top manager knows something he/she feels should not be divulged to the subordinate, such behavior may be appropriate. However, this would be most unusual, and there can be an expected cost in the form of dysfunctional behavior on the part of subordinates whose budgets were unilaterally adjusted. It is more a case of poor human relations than poor ethics. However, one can also make the case that asking subordinates to do the unachievable is unethical.

b.   She feels that you are playing a game with her. By her building in budgetary slack, which you will counter with more rigorous budgetary targets, she will be more able to achieve the desired results. It does seem to be a deceptive practice to employ budgetary slack and all parties involved should attempt to build an atmosphere that encourages accurate estimation.

c.   Understanding revenues will probably have an effect on the planning of other activities because if the firm expects lower revenues, it will probably reduce planned activities in other offices of the firm. For example, lower expected revenues may make it seem infeasible to upgrade the computer graphics hardware and software of the firm. Note: See <u>IMA Standards of Ethical Conduct for Management Accountants</u> for further guidance in answering this discussion question.

67.   a.   The new agreement with the airline's pilots accomplishes two things. First, it allows Southwest Airlines to maintain a cost advantage over its competitors. For this airline a cost advantage is critical because it competes on the basis of price. Secondly, the airline's agreement with the pilots allows for the pilots to acquire common stock in the company. Pilot ownership of stock is advantageous for the company because it makes the pilots consider the perspective of owners in actions they take. Specifically, it makes them conscious of costs and makes them more oriented to long-term competitive issues.

b.   The stock ownership and bonus plans are likely to have favorable quality effects. Because the plan will force pilots to think like owners, both quality consciousness and cost consciousness should be enhanced. The stock ownership plan should make the pilots more long-term oriented in the decisions they make. Because higher quality frequently leads to lower costs, the pursuit of increased efficiency and higher profits should induce the pilots to be more concerned about quality.

CHAPTER 8
CAPITAL ASSET SELECTION AND CAPITAL BUDGETING

Questions

1. A capital asset is an asset that provides benefits to the firm for more than one year. Capital assets are primarily distinguished from other assets in that they have longer lives, and they exist only to provide the capacity for the firm to produce, distribute and market goods.

3. The screening evaluation is used only to determine if a project meets some predetermined standard (net present value >0, for example). In simply meeting this criterion, the project is not necessarily going to be funded. To be funded, a project must be evaluated based on how it compares to other projects that have also passed the screening criterion. This comparison will involve preference criteria. The preference criteria may take into account nonfinancial data: safety considerations, legal requirements, public service obligations, etc. Also, the preference criteria will need to take into account that some projects are mutually exclusive, others are mutually inclusive, and yet others are independent.

5. Independent projects exist when the acceptance of one project does not imply either acceptance or rejection of the other projects: Examples of independent projects:
   1. Computerized accounting system, new production equipment.
   2. New product line, employee safety training program.
   3. New CAD or CAM equipment, R&D for product development.

7. The purpose of discounted cash flow analysis is to account for the opportunity cost of money for transactions that occur at different points in time. There is no opportunity cost associated with accounting accruals, only cash transactions. Accordingly, discounted cash flow analysis focuses only on those transactions in which an opportunity cost (interest) exists--cash transactions.

9. A timeline is simply a graphical display of all cash flows associated with a project. The timeline shows both the amount and the timing of the cash flows. It is a helpful tool in organizing or structuring discounted cash flow analysis. Use of a timeline helps prevent oversight of certain cash flows and facilitates the netting of cash flows that occur at a common point in time.

11. The payback period is the amount of time required for cash inflows to recoup the initial cost of an investment. Usually, no allowance is made for the time value of money in computing the payback period. This is one reason it is normally used only in conjunction with other methods. Another reason is that the payback method ignores all cash flows that occur after the payback period.

13. If the NPV = 0, then the projected return on the project is equal to the discount rate. If the NPV < 0, the project's expected return is below the firm's discount rate; and if the NPV > 0, the expected return exceeds the firm's discount rate.

15. The profitability index, PI, is a measure that provides more information about relative "profitability" of two projects that are of dissimilar size. The PI relates the present value of each project to its initial cost. The net present value measure provides no indication of the actual cost of each investment.

17. Unique to the IRR, two major weaknesses are: (1) the IRR ignores the dollar magnitude of alternative projects, and (2) projects with large cash outflows in the later years of their lives may generate multiple IRRs.

19. The accelerated depreciation method will result in recognition of the depreciation tax shield more quickly. Consequently, the tax benefit of the depreciation tax shield will be recouped faster and result in a higher present value.

21. Quality is changed within an organization by two key mechanisms: training and acquisition of higher technology. Because both of these mechanisms require cash outlays today, for benefits to be derived in future periods, they are properly analyzed in a capital budgeting framework.

23. They are often rejected because they generate comparably low discounted cash flow measures: IRR, NPV, and PI. These low measures are often attributable to a failure of the firm to adequately quantify the benefits of high technology. Although the benefits tend to be underestimated, the costs tend to be overestimated, because effects on efficiency and quality are overlooked.

25. The post-investment audit provides information about the reliability of the estimates that were used as a basis for justifying an investment. The post-investment feedback provides information about the judgment of the manager and information to improve the capital budgeting process. It also provides a basis for managerial control in that actual cash flows can be compared to projected cash flows.

27. The accounting rate of return is the only method which relies on accrual-based accounting information rather than cash flows. Net income is determined by both cash flows and noncash expenses and revenues. For example, depreciation is a noncash expense, and the gain recognized on the sale of an asset is a noncash revenue.

Exercises

29. a. payback = $120,000 ÷ $40,000 = <u>3</u> years for both projects

    Based on the payback criterion, the projects are equally desirable.

    b. The projects are not equally desirable, even though they have the same payback. Project B's life is a full year longer than project A's life. Thus, the sum of cash flows to be derived from Project B exceeds the sum from Project A. This indicates a need to use a secondary method to evaluate capital projects when the payback method is used.

31.

Time:	t0	t1	t2	t3	t4	t5
Amount	$(300,000)	$125,000	$125,000	$40,000	$40,000	$40,000

Cash flow Description	Time	Amount	Discount Factor	Present Value
Purchase machine	t0	$(300,000)	1.0000	$(300,000)
Cash inflow	t1	125,000	.9091	113,638
Cash inflow	t2	125,000	.8265	103,313
Cash inflow	t3	40,000	.7513	30,052
Cash inflow	t4	40,000	.6830	27,320
Cash inflow	t5	40,000	.6209	24,836
NPV				$ (841)

33. a. present value of cash inflows = $630,000 × 4.3553
    = $2,743,839; this is the maximum that the firm could pay and still have a non-negative NPV.

    b. $2,743,839 ÷ $630,000 = <u>4.36</u> years (rounded)

c.   The marketing manager might question the following: how sales of the licensed product would affect sales of other products, how sales would be affected at the end of the license agreement if the agreement is not renewed, how competitors might respond to the license agreement, and whether the estimates of sales of the licensed product are reasonable.

35. a.   PV of inflows = $12,000 × 4.1114 = $49,337
           PI = $49,337 ÷ $55,475 = .89

     b.   Discount factor of IRR = $55,475 ÷ $12,000 = 4.6229
           IRR(4.6229, 6 years) = 8%

           No, this is not an acceptable investment. Since the project has an internal rate of return of 8%, and a PI less than 1, it would have a negative NPV if 12% were used as the discount rate.

37. a.   **Straight-line method:**
           Annual depreciation = $1,500,000 ÷ 8 = $187,500
           Tax benefit = $187,500 × .40 = $75,000
           PV = $75,000 × 5.7466 = $430,995 (rounded)

     b.   **Alternative method:**
           $1,500,000 × .15 × .40 × .9259 = $ 83,331
           $1,500,000 × .22 × .40 × .8573 =   113,164
           $1,500,000 × .21 × .40 × .7938 =   100,019
           $1,500,000 × .21 × .40 × .7350 =   92,610
           $1,500,000 × .21 × .40 × .6806 =   85,756
               Total $474,880

           Note: these depreciation rates are ones specified under the U.S. federal tax system.

     c.   The company might choose the straight-line method. The straight-line method would defer more of the depreciation deductions to the later years of the project's life so that more benefit would be obtained from the rising tax rates.

     d.   Tax experts should be consulted. In particular, the company should consult with the tax department of an accounting firm that carefully tracks tax policy. Although no individual can always predict congressional actions to change tax laws, firms that monitor pending tax legislation and discussions in congressional committees have a better picture than others of future changes in tax laws.

39. a.   Tax: $44,000 - $9,000 = $35,000
          Financial Accounting: $44,000 - $22,000 = $22,000

     b.   Pretax cash flow = market value = $32,000

          Cash flow after taxes = Market value - taxes
                                = $32,000-[($32,000 - $9,000) ×.40]
                                = $22,800

41. Cost = $6,000 + $400 × annuity discount factor(48 periods, 1%)
     $6,000 + ($400 × 37.974) = $21,190

43. a.

Cash flow Description	Time	Amount	Discount Factor	Present Value
Purchase blender	t0	$(300,000)	1.0000	$(300,000)
Cost savings	t1-t10	50,000	6.1446	307,230
NPV				$ 7,230

     b. $307,230 ÷ $300,000 = 1.02 (rounded)

     c. $50,000 × discount factor = $300,000
          discount factor = 6.000(10-year annuity)
          IRR = approximately 10.5%

     d. $300,000 ÷ $50,000 = 6 years

     e.   change in net income = $50,000 - ($300,000 ÷ 10)
                               = $20,000
          ARR = $20,000 ÷ ($300,000 ÷ 2) = 13.33%

45. The written report should emphasize that the future revenues of
     firms are determined, in part, by actions taken in the present
     to develop new products and services. The development process
     is controlled by research and development programs which, in
     turn, are controlled by the capital budget.
          By developing a rigorous capital budgeting system,
     potential research and development projects would be critically
     examined and approved only if they met stated performance
     criteria. The performance criteria would include financial
     measures such as net present value or internal rate of return.
     By establishing the financial criteria at high levels, only
     the most profitable research and development projects, and
     those with the greatest likelihood of success, would be
     approved.

47. a. The benefits of a post-completion audit program for capital expenditure projects include

- The comparison of actual results with projected results to validate that a project is meeting expected performance or to take corrective action or terminate a project not achieving expected performance.

- An evaluation of the accuracy of projections from different departments.

- The improvement of future capital project revenue and cost estimates through analyzing variations between expected and actual results from previous projects and the motivational effect on personnel arising from the knowledge that a post audit will be done.

 b. Practical difficulties that would be encountered in collecting and accumulating information include

- Isolating the incremental changes caused by one capital project from all the other factors that change in a dynamic manufacturing and/or marketing environment.

- Identifying the impact of inflation on all costs in the capital project justification.

- Updating the original proposal for approval changes that may have occurred after the initial approval.

- Having a sufficiently sophisticated information accumulation system to measure actual costs incurred by the capital project.

- Allocating sufficient administrative time and expenses for the post-completion audit.

(CMA)

Problems

49. a. ($000s omitted)

	t0	t1	t2	t3	t4	t5	t6	t7	t8
Investment	-120								
New C.M.		33.0	33.0	33.0	33.0	33.0	33.0	33.0	33.0
Fixed costs		0	-7.4	-9.6	-9.6	-9.6	-9.9	-9.9	-9.9	-9.9
Annual flow	-120	25.6	23.4	23.4	23.4	23.1	23.1	23.1	23.1

 b.

Year	Cash savings	Cumulative savings
1	$25,600	$ 25,600
2	23,400	49,000
3	23,400	72,400
4	23,400	95,800
5	23,100	118,900

Payback = 5 + [($120,000 - $118,900) ÷ $23,100] = 5.05 years

c.

Time	Cash flow	PV factor for 10%	Present value
0	$(120,000)	1.0000	$(120,000)
1	25,600	.9091	23,273
2	23,400	.8265	19,340
3	23,400	.7513	17,580
4	23,400	.6830	15,982
5	23,100	.6209	14,343
6	23,100	.5645	13,040
7	23,100	.5132	11,855
8	23,100	.4665	10,776
NPV			$ 6,189

The NPV is acceptable. Note that a more conservative calculation of NPV would have assumed that the lease payments were made at the beginning of each year. This assumption would result in a reduction of the NPV.

51. a.   Pessimistic Scenario:

Cash flow Description	Time	Amount	Discount Factor	Present Value
Damage deposit	t0	$(2,000,000)	1.0000	$(2,000,000)
Relocation costs	t0	(200,000)	1.0000	(200,000)
Net cash inflow	t1	200,000	.9009	180,180
Net cash inflow	t2	200,000	.8116	162,320
Net cash inflow	t3	700,000	.7312	511,840
Reclamation costs	t4	(1,000,000)	.6587	(658,700)
Deposit refund	t4	2,000,000	.6587	1,317,400
NPV				$ (686,960)

Optimistic Scenario:

Cash flow Description	Time	Amount	Discount Factor	Present Value
Damage deposit	t0	$(2,000,000)	1.0000	$(2,000,000)
Relocation costs	t0	(200,000)	1.0000	(200,000)
Net cash inflow	t1	520,000	.9009	468,468
Net cash inflow	t2	520,000	.8116	422,032
Net cash inflow	t3	1,300,000	.7312	950,560
Reclamation costs	t4	(700,000)	.6587	(461,090)
Deposit refund	t4	2,000,000	.6587	1,317,400
NPV				$ 497,370

b.

$$\$(686,960) \times .3 = \$(206,088)$$
$$497,370 \times .7 = 348,159$$
$$\text{Expected NPV} \quad \$ 142,071$$

The company should accept the project because the expected overall NPV is positive.

53. a.

	Year 1	Year 2	Year 3	Year 4	Year 5	Years 6+
Receipts	$ 120,000	$240,000	$300,000	$360,000	$450,000	$540,000
Cash exp.	(150,000)	(150,000)	(155,000)	(205,000)	(200,000)	(245,000)
Depr.	(75,000)	(75,000)	(75,000)	(75,000)	(75,000)	(75,000)
Tax.Income	$(105,000)	$ 15,000	$ 70,000	$ 80,000	$175,000	$220,000
Taxes	36,750	(5,250)	(24,500)	(28,000)	(61,250)	(77,000)
Net income	$ (68,250)	$ 9,750	$ 45,500	$ 52,000	$113,750	$143,000
Depr.	75,000	75,000	75,000	75,000	75,000	75,000
CFAT	$ 6,750	$ 84,750	$120,500	$127,000	$188,750	$218,000

Cash flow Description	Time	Amount	Discount Factor	Present Value
Buy equipment	t0	$(600,000)	1.0000	$(600,000.00)
Working capital	t0	(300,000)	1.0000	(300,000.00)
Displays	t0	(150,000)	1.0000	(150,000.00)
Annual cash flow	t1	6,750	.9346	6,308.55
Annual cash flow	t2	84,750	.8734	74,020.65
Annual cash flow	t3	120,500	.8163	98,364.15
Annual cash flow	t4	127,000	.7629	96,888.30
Annual cash flow	t5	188,750	.7130	134,578.75
Annual cash flow	t6-t10	218,000	2.9234*	637,301.20
Salvage (after tax)	t10	16,250	.5084	8,261.50
Working capital	t10	300,000	.5084	152,520.00
NPV				$158,243.10

PI = $1,208,243.10 ÷ $1,050,000 = 1.15

*2.9234 = 7.0236(10 years, 7%) - 4.1002(5 years, 7%)

b.

	Amount	Cumulative
Year 1	$ 6,750	$ 6,750
Year 2	84,750	91,500
Year 3	120,500	212,000
Year 4	127,000	339,000
Year 5	188,750	527,750
Year 6	218,000	745,750
Year 7	218,000	963,750
Year 8	218,000	1,181,750

Payback = 7 years + (($1,050,000 - $963,750) ÷ $218,000)
         = 7.40 years

c.   Yes, it meets the criterion: NPV > 0; PI > 1.

d.   As an expert in income taxation, you would be able to
     recommend alternative treatments of depreciation, and
     project changes in tax rates or the tax law.

55. a. Annual cost savings from new technology:
Acid A: (40 - 10) × 750 × $2 = $45,000
Acid B: (20 - 5) × 750 × $2 = 22,500
Total annual cost savings $67,500

NPV calculation

Cash flow Description	time	Amount	Discount Factor	Present Value
Buy equipment	t0	$(500,000)	1.0000	$(500,000)
Annual cash flow	t1-t6	67,500	4.4859	302,798
NPV				$(197,202)

Based on the NPV criterion, the project is unacceptable.

b. Although the NPV indicates the project is unacceptable financially by a wide margin, there are other factors to be considered.

- By reducing the waste of acids A and B, the firm may not only save the disposal costs included in the calculation, but also the purchase costs of the quantity of each acid that is wasted under the existing technology.

- Disposal costs of the waste acids may rise to a level much higher than $2 in the future. It may be unreasonable to assume the costs will remain at this level.

- If the new technology reduces the quantity of acids to be purchased because of the reduction in waste, society may further benefit by a reduction in the quantity of harmful waste and by-products generated by Houston Chemical's suppliers of the acids.

- If the volume of the chemical solvent produced increases in the future, the amount of savings generated by the new technology would be greater than estimated assuming constant future demand.

- By reducing its level of waste, the company may avoid future fines, penalties, and legal judgments that may be enforceable in the present but result from the generation of these harmful materials. For example, if the firm that is responsible for disposing of these acids acts improperly and causes environmental damage, Houston Chemical could be held liable for any resulting cleanup costs.

57. a. Initial cost = $(87,500) + $(2,500) + $25,000 = $(65,000)
Net annual cash flow
Labor savings ($15,000 - $12,500) $ 2,500
Other savings ($24,000 - $10,000)   14,000
Revenue (250,000 - 200,000) × $.15   7,500
Total $24,000

NPV = ($24,000 × 5.2161) - $65,000 = $60,186

The NPV indicates this is an acceptable project.

b. Payback = $65,000 ÷ $24,000 = <u>2.71</u> years

c. Incremental income = incremental income - incremental depreciation
    = $24,000 - $6,250 = $17,750

ARR = $17,750 ÷ ($65,000 ÷ 2) = <u>54.62%</u>

The ARR far exceeds the minimum required return of 14%.

Cases

59. a. Purchase:
    NPV = -$500,000 + ($21,428.57 × 5.2064)
        = -$500,000 + $111,565.71
        = <u>-$388,434.29</u>

    Depreciation expense per year:
    ($500,000 ÷ 7) × .30 = <u>$21,428.57</u>

    Lease:
    NPV = -($70,000 × 3.9927) - [$7,000 × (5.2064 - 3.9927)]
        = -$279,489 - $8,496
        = <u>-$287,985</u>

    Lease payments reimbursement: first 5 years (-$100,000 × .30), $30,000; last 2 years (-$10,000 × .30), $3,000
    Based on NPV, the board should lease the CAT scanner.

b. NPV of purchase remains the same.
    NPV of leasing:
    NPV = -($100,000 × 4.3121) + ($30,000 × 3.9927) -
          [$10,000 × (5.6229 - 4.3121)] + [$3,000 × (5.2064
          - 3.9927)]
        = -$444,318 + $123,422
        = <u>-$320,896</u>

    The board should still lease the machine.

c. Purchase alternative:
    $500,000 - ($500,000 × .05) = $475,000
    ($475,000 ÷ 7) × .30 = $20,357

    NPV = -$500,000 + ($20,357 × 5.2064) + ($25,000 × .5835)
        = <u>-$379,426</u>
    Lease alternative remains the same as Part a; board should select leasing.

d. Calculation for purchase: same as Part c.
    Calculation for lease: same as Part b.
    Board should select lease alternative.

61. Note: Students may have slightly different answers. The CMA solution uses only two-digit present value factors.

 a. Present Value Analysis (using 6%)

	Initial Outlay	2000	2001	2002	2003	2004
Internal Financing						
Outlay	($1,000,000)					
Depr. tax shield		$160,000	$ 96,000	$ 57,600	$ 43,200	$ 43,200
Net CF	($1,000,000)	$160,000	$ 96,000	$ 57,600	$ 43,200	$ 43,200
PV factors	1.00	0.94	0.89	0.84	0.79	0.75
NPV	($1,000,000)	$150,400	$ 85,440	$ 48,384	$ 34,128	$ 32,400
Bank Loan						
Outlay	($100,000)					
Loan payment		($237,420)	($237,420)	($237,420)	($237,420)	($237,420)
Interest tax shield		36,000	30,103	23,617	16,482	8,638
Depr. tax shield		$160,000	$ 96,000	$ 57,600	$ 43,200	$ 43,200
Net CF	($100,000)	($ 41,420)	($111,317)	($156,203)	($177,738)	($185,582)
PV factors	1.00	0.94	0.89	0.84	0.79	0.75
NPV	($100,000)	($ 38,935)	($ 99,072)	($131,211)	($140,413)	($139,187)
Lease						
Outlay	($ 50,000)					
Tax shield on outlay		$ 20,000				
Payments net of tax ($220,000 × 60%)		($132,000)	($132,000)	($132,000)	($132,000)	($132,000)
NCF	($ 50,000)	($112,000)	($132,000)	($132,000)	($132,000)	($132,000)
PV factors	1.00	0.94	0.89	0.84	0.79	0.75
NPV	($ 50,000)	($105,280)	($117,480)	($110,880)	($104,280)	($ 99,000)

 NPV for internal financing = $649,248
 NPV for bank loan = $648,818
 NPV for lease = $586,920

Supporting calculations

Depreciation tax shield

Year	Depreciation	Rate	Tax shield
1	$1,000,000 × .40 = $400,000	× .40 =	$160,000
2	($1,000,000-$400,000) × .40 = 240,000	× .40 =	96,000
3	($1,000,000-$640,000) × .40 = 144,000	× .40 =	57,600
4	($1,000,000-$784,000) × .50 = 108,000	× .40 =	43,200
5	($1,000,000-$784,000) × .50 = 108,000	× .40 =	43,200

Interest tax shield

Year	Interest	Rate	Tax shield
1	$90,000	.40	$36,000
2	75,258	.40	30,103
3	59,042	.40	23,617
4	41,204	.40	16,482
5	21,596	.40	8,638

1. Metrohealth should employ the cost of debt of six percent (which represents the after-tax effect of the ten percent incremental borrowing rate) as a discount rate in calculating the net present value for all three financing alternatives.

   Investment decisions (accept versus reject) and financing decisions should be separated. Cost of capital or hurdle rates apply to investment decisions but not to financing decisions. This application is a financing decision. Incremental cost of debt is the basic rate used for discounting in financing decisions because the assumption made is that the firm would have no idle cash available for funding and would have to borrow from an outside lending institution at the incremental borrowing rate (10 percent in this case).

2. The financing alternative most advantageous to Metrohealth is leasing. This alternative has the lowest net present value ($586,920) when compared to the other two alternatives.

b. Some qualitative factors Paul Monden should include for management consideration before deciding on the financing alternatives are:

   ■ The differential impact from one financing method versus another for equipment acquisitions due to various health care, third-party payor, reimbursement scenarios (the federal government with DRG reimbursement or insurance company reimbursement).

   ■ The technology of the equipment along with the risk of technological obsolescence. If major technological advances are expected, the preferred qualitative choice would be leasing from a lessor who would absorb any loss due to equipment obsolescence.

   ■ The maintenance agreement included in the operating lease.

(CMA)

Ethics and Quality Discussion

63.   a.   Rachel Arnett's revision of her first proposal can be
          considered a violation of the Standards of Ethical
          Conduct. She discarded her reasonable projections and
          estimates after she was questioned by William Earle. She
          used figures that had a remote chance of occurring. By
          doing this, she violated the Standard of Objectivity--
          "Communicate information fairly and objectively" and
          "disclose fully relevant information that could reasonably
          be expected to influence an intended user's understanding
          of the reports, comments, and recommendations presented."
          By altering her analysis, she also violated the Standard
          of Integrity. She engaged in an activity that would
          prejudice her ability to carry out her duties ethically,
          and she failed to communicate unfavorable as well as
          favorable information and professional judgments or
          opinions. In addition, she violated the Standard of
          Competence--"prepare complete and clear reports and
          recommendations after appropriate analysis for relevant
          and reliable information."

      b.   Earle was clearly in violation of the Standards of Ethical
          Conduct for Management Accountants because he tried to
          persuade a subordinate to prepare a proposal with data
          that were false and misleading. Earle has violated the
          Standards of Competence (failure to perform professional
          duties in accordance with technical standards, prepare
          complete and clear reports and recommendations after
          appropriate analyses of relevant and reliable
          information), Integrity (engaged in an activity that would
          prejudice his ability to carry out his duties ethically,
          actively or passively subvert the attainment of the
          organization's legitimate and ethical objectives, failure
          to communicate unfavorable as well as favorable
          information and professional judgments or opinions, and
          supported activity that would discredit the profession),
          and Objectivity (failed to communicate information fairly
          and objectively and did not disclose fully all relevant
          information that could reasonably be expected to influence
          an intended user's understanding of the reports, comments,
          and recommendations presented).

      c.   The elements of the projection and estimation process that
          are compromised because of a predetermined, misleading
          outcome include
          ■   The quality of the base data.
          ■   The quality of the assumptions used.
          ■   The probability of the projection occurring.
          ■   The credibility of the people submitting the
              projection.

d.   The internal controls Fore Corporation could implement to prevent unethical behavior include

- Approval of all formal capital expenditure proposals by the Controller and/or the Board of Directors.

- Designating a non-accounting/finance manager to coordinate capital expenditure requests or segregating duties during the preparation and approval of capital expenditure requests.

- Requiring all capital expenditure proposals be reviewed by senior operating management, which includes the Controller, before the proposals are submitted for approval.

- Requiring the internal audit staff to review all capital expenditure proposals or contracting external auditors to review the proposal if the corporation lacks personnel.

(CMA)

CHAPTER 9
INTRODUCTION TO A STANDARD COST SYSTEM

Questions

1. A standard costing system is a planning tool because it ties in with the organization's financial budgets. The standard costs represent an expectation about what actual costs should be. The standard costing system's contribution to organizational control involves the comparison of the actual costs incurred for a period to the standard costs. Managers will investigate substantial deviations between actual and standard costs and take actions to bring them into alignment.

3. Standards are necessary for each cost component of a product or service so that the most detailed variance analysis can be conducted. Standards for the monetary amount and quantity of each cost component allow separate comparisons to actual figures and provide managers with the best means of determining what went "wrong" or "right" during the period. Such determinations are critical to correcting problems or instituting new methodologies for improvement.

5. Standard costing would provide the greatest cost control benefits. Standard costing requires the firm to develop standards or budgets for all three product cost pools. Such standards can then be compared to the actual costs generated for a period. Alternatively, an actual costing system does not require the firm to develop a standard. Accordingly, there is no baseline against which actual costs can be compared to achieve control.

7. A bill of materials provides information about the physical description of items and the quantity needed to produce one unit of product. It presents material components of a product, their specifications (including quality), and minimum quantities need to produce a unit. It is used in a standard cost system to help in developing a standard cost card that contains the similar quantity information adjusted for expected waste and/or spoilage as well as costs.

9. A predetermined overhead rate is considered a standard because that rate has been developed as the accepted basis on which to assign overhead using an appropriate activity driver. Thus, it represents the "norm" per unit of activity measure.

11. This statement is false. Although consideration should be
     given to the ease of obtaining a measurement in the production
     area, overhead standards should be set first on the basis of
     the most reasonable cost driver. If this measure is the most
     logical but is unavailable, accounting and data processing
     personnel should work together to determine a method of data
     collection.

13. Computing the variance based on the quantity purchased is
     consistent with recognizing the variance at the earliest time.
     Because the variance is known as soon as there is agreement
     with the vendor on the terms of the purchase, it can be
     recognized at the moment the firm has made the commitment to
     buy the material.

15. Possible causes of the unfavorable material quantity variance
     could include the following:
     · the material is old and deteriorated;
     · the material is the wrong grade or quality;
     · the machinery used to cut the material needs to be serviced;
     · the material is being introduced into the process at the
       wrong time;
     · the employees are careless or poorly trained;
     · someone is stealing material;
     · the standards were set incorrectly; or
     · errors in accounting are being made for the purchase or use
       of materials.

17. The positive analysis of this variance is that your employees
     work very quickly. The negative analysis of this variance is
     that your workers may not be providing the best service. By
     not having some linkage between service quality and direct
     labor time, workers may simply work fast--not caring about
     whether things are being done correctly.

19. Managers view capacity utilization as a measure of
     productivity. In addition, capacity utilization may focus on
     the need for fewer or additional resources to be spent on
     plant assets. If a plant is consistently operating at a
     significant volume under its normal capacity, the firm may
     have too many dollars invested in physical plant; if the plant
     is consistently operating above normal capacity, there may be
     a need for additional investment in facilities.
         Managers are not controlling costs when they control
     utilization; these are separate aspects of the fixed overhead
     question. Cost control arises when physical facilities are
     acquired and costs are committed, while the control of
     utilization arises during production.

21. a.   The material price variance can be calculated at point of purchase or point of use and is the responsibility of the purchasing agent. Firms using traditional inventory management techniques will probably compute the variance based on quantity purchased. Firms that have adopted just-in-time (JIT) techniques will prefer to compute the variance based on the quantity used so that there will be no incentive to purchase materials for which there is no current production need.

   b.   The material quantity variance should be calculated at point of issuance of materials. This variance is typically the responsibility of the production supervisor and should be noted through the use of excess material requisition slips.

   c. & d.   The labor rate and labor efficiency variances should be computed as payroll is recorded or assigned to Work in Process Inventory. These variances are also normally the responsibility of the production supervisor.

   e.   The variable overhead spending variance is usually calculated at the end of the month or the end of an accounting period. The variable overhead spending variance is primarily the responsibility of the production support personnel using the resources-- especially if resources have been wasted.

   f.   The volume variance is usually calculated at the end of the month or the end of an accounting period. The volume variance is the responsibility of the production supervisor who controls scheduling. Some amount of volume variance may be planned for, depending on demand.
        Although the above assignments of responsibility are the usual ones, there may be exceptions. Some variances are interrelated, such as an unfavorable material quantity variance caused by inferior material quality and an unfavorable labor efficiency variance caused by reworking items made from the low-quality material. Labor rates may not be under the control of the production supervisor, but possibly the result of a new labor contract. Managers must look for underlying relationships when investigating both favorable and unfavorable variances.

23.   Updating standards is important so that those standards can be used as a reasonable approximation of actual costs on the financial statements. Current standards are also important because management's planning, controlling, decision making, and performance evaluations would be less effective if based on out-of-date standards.

25.   If the variances are insignificant, they are closed to Cost of
      Goods Sold or Cost of Services Rendered. This disposition is
      acceptable because the cost-benefit criterion would not
      support the time and effort that allocation to related
      accounts would take.

Exercises

27.   a.   Material price variance = 105,600 pounds × ($2.40 -
           $2.25) = $15,840 U

      b.   Standard quantity allowed = 225 statues × 420 pounds =
           94,500 pounds
           Material quantity variance = $2.25(99,400 - 94,500) =
           $11,025 U

      c.   An unfavorable price variance could be caused by
           suppliers in general deciding to reduce output and, thus,
           causing prices to increase (consider, for example, the
           decision in Spring 1998 by OPEC to cut output because the
           price of oil was too low). Three other possibilities are
           that the purchasing agent bought the material from a
           vendor different from that contacted when the standard
           was set, that the standard was out-of-date, or that there
           was a rush order for the material which created an
           expediting charge.

29.   a.   Material price variance based on quantity purchased:
           1,000,000 × ($.037 - $.039) = $2,000 F
           Material quantity variance = $.039 × (780,000 - 794,000)
           = $546 F

      b.   A theoretical standard is based on the presumption of no
           inefficiencies of any type (whether human or machine); it
           would provide for the maximum level of activity from any
           input resource. A practical standard can be reached or
           slightly exceeded with reasonable effort 60 percent to 70
           percent of the time; this standard allows for normal,
           unavoidable problems. An expected standard reflects what
           is actually expected to occur and, thus, variances from
           it should be minimal; it anticipates future waste and
           inefficiencies and allows for them.

      c.   A change to theoretical standards would not affect any
           monetary variances (such as price, rate, or spending).
           Such a change would only affect variances related to
           activity (such as quantity, efficiency, or volume).

31.   a.   Total actual payroll = 41,250 × $7.25 = $299,062.50

      b.   Labor rate variance = 41,250($7.25 - $6.75) = $20,625 U

      c.   Labor efficiency variance = $6.75(41,250 - 40,500) =
           $5,062.50 U

33. a. Standard time allowed = 1,200 bookcases × 7 DLHs = 8,400
         DLHs

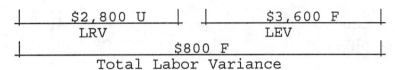

AP × AQ	SP × AQ	SP × SQ
$? × 8,000	$9 × 8,000	$9 × 8,400
$74,800	$72,000	$75,600

         | $2,800 U | | $3,600 F |
                   LRV   LEV
         | $800 F |
                      Total Labor Variance

     b. The actual pay rate per hour is $9.35 ($74,800 ÷ 8,000).
         Two possible options exist: (1) the increase in pay made
         the workers more enthusiastic about their job and, thus,
         work harder; or (2) more highly skilled workers were used
         who cost more, but worked faster.

35. a. Standard quantity allowed = (1,800 units × 15 minutes) ÷
         60 minutes per hour = 450 MHs
         Total applied VOH = $14 × 450 MHs = $6,300

     b. Actual VOH   SP × AQ   Applied VOH
                           $14 × 410 $14 × 450
         $6,200 $5,740 $6,300

         | $460 U | | $560 F |
            VOH Sp. Var.   VOH Eff. Var.
         | $100 F |
                        Total VOH Variance

     c. It is possible that the standard quantity of machine time
         is obsolete and needs to be changed to reflect new skills
         by workers, new machine technology, or new factory
         layout.

37. a. Total monthly budgeted FOH ÷ Expected capacity =
         Predetermined FOH rate; thus, Expected capacity ×
         Predetermined FOH rate = Total monthly budgeted FOH:
         3,000 DLHs × $2 per DLH = $6,000

     b. Total standard DLHs = (100 × 10) + (400 × 3) + (60 × 12)
         = 2,920 DLHs
         Total applied FOH = $2 × 2,920 = $5,840

     c. Actual FOH   Budgeted FOH   Applied FOH
                           $2 × 3,000 $2 × 2,920
         $6,100 $6,000 $5,840

         | $100 U | | $160 U |
            FOH Sp. Var.   Volume Var.
         | $260 U |
                        Total FOH Variance

d.   The volume variance addresses the issue of the capacity
     used to determine the fixed overhead application rate
     compared to the standard quantity allowed for the actual
     production of the period. In this case, Nadia Co.
     expected to utilize 3,000 DLHs producing a selection of
     tables, chairs, and desks. The standard DLHs for the
     actual production was 2,920. Thus, 80 DLHs that had been
     expected to be worked were not, resulting in an
     underapplication of $2 × 80 DLHs or $160 of fixed
     overhead.

39.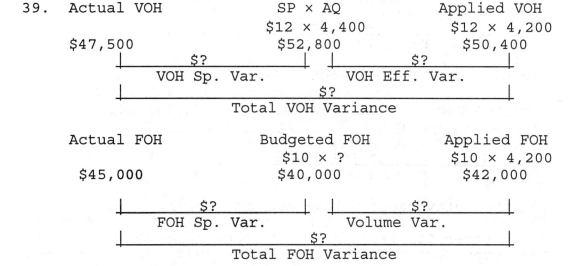

a.   Total actual overhead cost = Actual VOH + Actual FOH =
     $47,500 + $45,000 = $92,500

b.   Total applied overhead = Applied VOH + Applied FOH =
     ($12 × 4,200) + ($10 × $4,200) = $50,400 + $42,000 =
     $92,400

c.   VOH spending variance = $47,500 - $52,800 = $5,300 F
     VOH efficiency variance = $52,800 - $50,400 = $2,400 U
     Total VOH variance = $2,900 F

d.   FOH spending variance = $45,000 - $40,000 = $5,000 U
     Volume variance = $40,000 - $42,000 = $2,000 F
     Total FOH variance = $3,000 U

41. Standard quantity of time allowed = (399,000 × 20 minutes) ÷ 60 minutes = 133,000 MHs

    Because the company can make 3 units in an hour, the variable overhead rate per MH is $4 per unit multiplied by 3 or $12 per MH. The fixed overhead rate per MH is $15 (or $5 × 3).

    a.   Actual VOH   SP × AQ   Applied VOH
                              $12 × 130,000 $12 × 133,000
            $2,100,000 $1,560,000 $1,596,000
                 | $540,000 U | | $36,000 F |
                    VOH Sp. Var.   VOH Eff. Var.
                 | $504,000 U |
                         Total VOH Variance

    b.   Actual FOH   Budgeted FOH   Applied FOH
                              $15 × 200,000 $15 × 133,000
            $4,500,000 $3,000,000 $1,995,000
                 | $1,500,000 U | | $1,005,000 U |
                    FOH Sp. Var.   Volume Var.
                 | $2,505,000 U |
                         Total FOH Variance

    c. No, the unfavorable volume variance is not a valid measure of capacity utilization. In fact, it would have been better for Titanic Inc. if the volume variance had been even more unfavorable--because that would have meant that the company would have produced even fewer units. Given that sales were so low, the company needs to either store all the excess production, sell it as a substantially reduced price, give it away, or remelt the plastic if possible and use it as raw material for another product.

43. a. Raw Material Inventory   600,000
       Material Price Variance   3,700
           Accounts Payable   603,700

    b. Work in Process Inventory   552,000
           Raw Material Inventory   542,900
           Material Quantity Variance   9,100

    c. Work in Process Inventory   288,000
       Labor Efficiency Variance   3,900
           Wages Payable   289,800
           Labor Rate Variance   2,100

    d. Material Quantity Variance   9,100
       Labor Rate Variance   2,100
           Material Price Variance   3,700
           Labor Efficiency Variance   3,900
           Cost of Goods Sold   3,600

Problems

45. a.   Standard quantity of material allowed = 32,000 pendants
    × 1/8 pound per pendant = <u>4,000 pounds</u>

    b. $744 F material quantity variance ÷ $6.20 = 120 pounds
    less than standard quantity allowed
    Actual quantity of material used = 4,000 - 120 = <u>3,880
    pounds</u>

    c.   Actual quantity of material purchased = Actual quantity
    used + 800 pounds = 3,880 + 800 = <u>4,680 pounds</u>

    d.   Standard price of material purchased = 4,680 pounds ×
    $6.20 = $29,016
    Actual price of material purchased = Standard cost of
    material purchased minus the favorable price variance
    = $29,016 - $1,235 = <u>$27,781</u> or $5.94 per pound

    e.   Standard hours allowed for production = (32,000 pendants
    × 15 minutes) ÷ 60 = <u>8,000 DLHs</u>

    f.   Total standard direct labor cost = $12 × 8,000 DLHs =
    $96,000
    Budgeted direct labor cost for actual hours worked = $12
    × 8,200 = $98,400
    Labor efficiency variance = $98,400 - $96,000 = <u>$2,400 U</u>

    g.   Total labor variance = Labor rate variance + Labor
    efficiency variance: $1,700 U = LRV + $2,400 U; LRV =
    <u>$700 F</u>

    h.   Actual labor cost = Budgeted labor cost - Favorable
    labor rate variance = $98,400 - $700 = $97,700
    Actual labor rate paid = Actual labor cost ÷ Actual
    labor hours = $97,700 ÷ 8,200 = <u>$11.91 per DLH</u>

47.

	Case 1	Case 2	Case 3	Case 4
Units produced	600	(d)	320	1,250
Std. hours per unit	2	.6	(g)	(j)
Std. hours allowed	(a)	600	480	(k)
Std. rate per hour	$6	(e)	$5.50	$8
Act. hours worked	1,230	580	(h)	5,100
Act. labor cost	(b)	(f)	$1,656.80	$30,600
LRV	$246 U	$290 U	$15.20 F	(l)
LEV	(c)	$80 F	(i)	$600 U

a. Standard hours allowed = 600 × 2 = <u>1,200 DLHs</u>

b. Actual labor cost: Actual hours worked × Standard rate =
1,230 × $6 = $7,380 budgeted labor cost; $7,380 + $246
unfavorable labor rate variance = <u>$7,626</u>

c. Labor efficiency variance = $6 × (1,230 - 1,200) = <u>$180 U</u>

d. Units produced = 600 ÷ .6 = <u>1,000 units</u>

e. Standard rate per hour: Labor efficiency variance =
Standard   rate × (Actual hours - Standard hours
allowed); $80 F = ?(580 - 600) = <u>$4 per DLH</u>

f. Actual labor cost: Budgeted labor cost + Unfavorable
labor rate variance = (580 × $4) + $290 U = <u>$2,610</u>

g. Standard hours per unit = 480 ÷ 320 = <u>1.5 hours</u>

h. Actual hours worked: Budgeted labor cost for actual
hours worked = (Actual labor cost + favorable labor
rate variance) = ($1,656.80 + $15.20) = $1,672; Actual
hours worked = Budgeted labor cost ÷ Standard rate =
$1,672 ÷ $5.50 = <u>304 DLHs</u>

i. Labor efficiency variance = $5.50 × (304 - 480) = <u>$968 F</u>

k. (Must do before part j)
Standard hours allowed: Budgeted cost at actual hours -
Unfavorable labor efficiency variance = Total standard
cost; (5,100 × $8) - $600 = $40,800 - $600 = $40,200;
$40,200 ÷ $8 = <u>5,025 DLHs</u>

j. Standard hours per unit = 5,025 ÷ 1,250 = <u>4.02 DLHs</u>

l. Labor rate variance = $30,600 - $40,800 = <u>$10,200 F</u>

49.   a.   **Conventional Approach**
             Direct Labor Efficiency Variance = (Actual hours -
             Standard hours) × Standard DL cost per hour = [5,800 -
             (5 hours × 1,200 units produced] × $20 = $4,000 F
             Direct Labor Rate Variance = (Actual DL cost per hour -
             Standard DL cost per hour) × Actual DLHs = [($22 -
             $20) × 5,800] = $11,600 U
             Total Direct Labor Variance: $4,000 F - $11,600 U =
             $7,600 U

             Logical Approach
             Direct Labor Efficiency Variance = (Actual hours -
             Standard hours) × Standard DL cost per hour = [5,800 -
             (5 hours × 1,200 units produced] × $20 = $4,000 F
             Direct Labor Rate Variance = (Actual DL cost per hour -
             Standard DL cost per hour) × Standard DLHs = [($22 -
             $20) × 6,000] = $12,000 U
             Direct Labor Joint Variance = (Actual DL cost per hour -
             Standard DL cost per hour) × (Actual DLHs - Standard
             DLHs) = [($22 - $20) × (5,800 - 6,000] = $400 F
             Total Direct Labor Variance: $4,000 F + $400 F - $12,000
             U = $7,600 U

       b.   The difference is in the treatment of the labor rate
             variance. The second approach determines a rate variance
             based on standard hours allowed (6,000 DLHs) and a joint
             variance caused by simultaneously having a difference in
             rate ($2) and a difference in usage (200 SLHs). Although
             this latter approach gives a little more information, it
             may often be more of a distraction than it is worth. It
             is a matter of management preference as to whether
             accountants provide the data on the impact on the total
             variance caused by a combined rate and a usage difference
             from the standards. Most choose not to make this
             refinement.
                        [IMA adapted. Copyright 1990 IMA (formerly NAA)]

51. a.   Budgeted annual fixed overhead = 1,600 billable hours
per month × $15 per hour × 12 months = $288,000

   b.

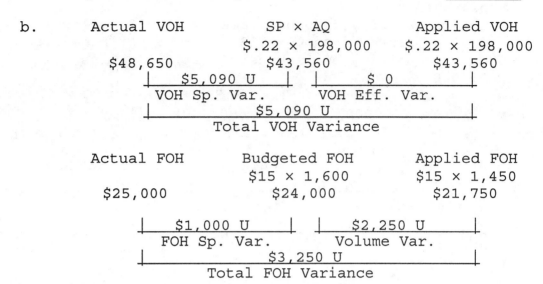

Actual VOH	SP × AQ	Applied VOH
	$.22 × 198,000	$.22 × 198,000
$48,650	$43,560	$43,560

$5,090 U	$ 0
VOH Sp. Var.	VOH Eff. Var.

$5,090 U
Total VOH Variance

Actual FOH	Budgeted FOH	Applied FOH
	$15 × 1,600	$15 × 1,450
$25,000	$24,000	$21,750

$1,000 U	$2,250 U
FOH Sp. Var.	Volume Var.

$3,250 U
Total FOH Variance

   c.   The variable overhead efficiency variance is zero because
there is no standard quantity of pages. Had the firm set
a standard of X number of pages per billable hour, there
might have been an efficiency variance.

Bases other than pages of documentation that might
be more useful drivers of variable overhead might include
a proportion of secretarial time to attorney billable
time and a proportion of hours of research time to
attorney billable time. The problem with any such
quantity standard in a law firm is that the cases being
handled may be so diverse that a norm cannot be set. This
might not be true, however, if the law firm worked only
on specific types of cases; for instance, if the law firm
did only tax work, standard quantities of time could be
set for the preparation of different types of tax
returns, or for tax planning under certain differing
estate value amount.

53. a.   Standard quantity of lumber = 11,000 tables × 60 board
          feet = 660,000; standard cost = $54 ÷ 60 = $.90 per
          board foot
          Standard quantity of pipe frames = 11,000 tables × 2 =
          22,000; standard cost = $18 ÷ 2 = $9 per pipe frame
          Standard quantity of fasteners = 11,000 tables × 1 =
          11,000

	AQ × AP	AQ × SP	SQ × SP
Lumber	($.85 × 690,000)	($.90 × 690,000)	($.90 × 660,000)
Pipe	($9.10 × 22,250)	($9 × 22,250)	($9 × 22,000)
Fasteners	($6.90 × 11,120)	($8 × 11,120)	($8 × 11,000)
	$865,703	$910,210	$880,000

|_____ $44,507 F _____|_____ $30,210 U _____|
                MPV   MQV

Standard quantity of time allowed = 11,000 × .5 = 5,500
DLHs

AP × AQ	SP × AQ	SP × SQ
$14.20 × 5,600	$14 × 5,600	$14 × 5,500
$79,520	$78,400	$77,000

|_____ $1,120 U _____|_____ $1,400 U _____|
              LRV   LEV

Standard quantity of time allowed = 11,000 × 1/5 = 2,200
MHs

Actual VOH	SP × AQ	Applied VOH
	$20 × 2,000	$20 × 2,200
$38,000	$40,000	$44,000

|_____ $2,000 _____|_____ $4,000 F _____|
        VOH Sp. Var.   VOH Eff. Var.

Actual FOH	Budgeted FOH	Applied FOH
		$15 × 2,200
$32,300	$30,000	$33,000

|_____ $2,300 U _____|_____ $3,000 F _____|
        FOH Sp. Var.   Volume Var.

55. a.

Actual VCC	SP × AQ	Applied VCC
	$14 × 5,800	$14 × 6,000
$75,400	$81,200	$84,000

|_____ $5,800 F _____|_____ $2,800 F _____|
        VCC Sp. Var.   VCC Eff. Var.
|_____ $8,600 F _____|
               Total VCC Variance

Actual FCC	Budgeted FCC	Applied FCC
	$20 × 5,000	$20 × 6,000
$102,500	$100,000	$120,000

|_____ $2,500 U _____|_____ $20,000 F _____|
        FCC Sp. Var.   FCC Volume Var.
|_____ $17,500 F _____|
               Total FCC Variance

b. An annual computation of variances is not useful to managers because it does not provide any opportunity to correct problems as they arise or to encourage the adoption of positive techniques that serve to reduce costs or quantities. This is especially true in a highly automated environment (one that might be using a conversion cost category rather than the traditional labor and overhead ones); if something in an automated system is "out of control," it is essential that corrections take place as quickly as possible to prevent a continuation of the problem that might not be visible to machine operators and/or to avoid damaging sensitive automated equipment.

Cases

57. a. Direct material
      Raspberries (7.5 quarts* × $.80) $6.00
      Other ingredients (10 gallons × $.45)   4.50 $10.50
    Direct labor
      Sorting [(3 minutes × 6 quarts) ÷ 60) × $9]$2.70
      Blending [(12 minutes ÷ 60) × $9]   1.80   4.50
    Packaging (40 quarts** × $.38)   15.20
    Standard cost per 10-gallon batch $30.20
    *6 quarts × 5/4 = 7.5 quarts required to obtain 6 acceptable quarts
    **4 quarts per gallon × 10 gallons = 40 quarts

   b. 1. In general, the purchasing manager is held responsible for unfavorable material price variances. Causes of these variances include the following:
         · Failure to correctly forecast price increases.
         · Purchasing nonstandard or uneconomical lots.
         · Purchasing from suppliers other than those offering the most favorable terms.

      2. In general, the production manager or supervisor is held responsible for unfavorable labor efficiency variances. Causes of these variances include the following:
         · Poorly trained labor.
         · Substandard or inefficient equipment.
         · Inadequate supervision.

c.   One of the big factors affecting the quality of the
     raspberries is the weather. Thus, if one were able to
     understand exactly how weather conditions influenced the
     quality of the raspberry crop and if one could forecast
     the seasonal weather with some accuracy, a quantity
     standard could be developed that would be sensitive to
     the influence of weather on raspberry quality. This would
     allow the management to evaluate the actual quantity of
     raspberries used against a more relevant benchmark.

                                                         (CMA)

59. a.   1.   Revising the standards immediately would facilitate
               their use in a master budget. Use of revised
               standards would minimize production coordination
               problems and facilitate cash planning. Revised
               standards would facilitate more meaningful cost-
               volume-profit analysis and result in simpler, more
               meaningful variance analysis. Standards are often
               used in decision analysis such as make-or-buy,
               product pricing, or product discontinuance. The use
               of obsolete standards would impair such analysis.

          2.   Standard costs are carried through the accounting
               system in a standard cost system. Retaining the
               current standards and expanding the analysis of
               variances would eliminate the need to make changes
               in the accounting system.
                    Changing standards could have an adverse
               psychological impact on the persons using them.
               Retaining the current standards would preserve the
               well-known benchmarks and allow for consistency in
               reporting variances throughout the year. Variances
               are often computed and ignored. Retaining the
               current standards and expanding the analysis of
               variances would force a diagnosis of the costs and
               would increase the likelihood that significant
               variances would be investigated.

     b.   1.   Change in prime cost per unit because of the use of
               new direct material: (New material price - Old
               material price) × New material quantity = ($7.77 -
               $7.00) × 1 pound = $ .77 U
               Changes in prime cost because of the effect of
               direct material quality on direct material usage:
               (Old material quantity - New material quantity) ×
               Old material price = (1.25 pounds - 1.00 pound) ×
               $7.00 = $1.75 F
               Change in prime cost because of the effect of
               direct material quality on direct labor usage =
               (Old labor time - New labor time) × Old labor
               rate = (24/60 - 22/60) × $12.60 = $.42 F
               Total change in prime cost per unit because of the
               use of new direct material = $.77 U + $1.75 F +
               $.42 F = $1.40 F

2. Change in prime cost per unit because of the new labor contract: (New labor rate - Old labor rate) × New labor time = ($14.40 - $12.60) × 22/60 = $.66 U

Total reduction of prime cost per unit = $1.40 F - $.66 U = $.74 F

(CMA)

61. a. 1. The major advantages of using a standard cost system include
    · budgeting. Standard costs can be the building blocks for budget preparation and allow the development of flexible budgeting.
    · performance evaluation. Comparisons of actual costs to standard costs facilitate evaluation of the performance at the company, department, activity center, or individual level. Standards also allow employees to more clearly understand what is expected of them.

2. The disadvantages that can result from using a standard cost system include the following:
    · Cost standards that are too tight can have negative behavioral implications that may cause a decrease in motivation.
    · Standards may ignore qualitative characteristics that may jeopardize product quality.

b. 1. A standard cost system must be supported by top management to be successful. The parties who should participate in the standard-setting process include all levels of the organization, such as purchasing, engineering, production, and cost accounting. The value of their participation is that they are more likely to accept the standards as evaluation criteria.

2. The general features and characteristics associated with the introduction and operation of a standard cost system that make it an effective tool for cost control include the following:
    · Standard setting can be a participatory process with those individuals most familiar with the variables associated with standard setting available to provide the most accurate information. This sense of participation will help establish the legitimacy of the standards and give the participants a greater feeling of being part of the operation.
    · Standards that are set for routine activities, that can be identifiable and measurable, and associated with specific cost factors of uniform products in long production runs.
    · Standards promote cost control through the use of variance analysis and performance reports.

c. The consequences of having the standards set by an outside consulting firm include the following:
- There could be negative employee reaction as the employees did not participate in the standard-setting process.
- There could be dissatisfaction if the standards contain cost elements that are not controllable by the production groups but they are held responsible for unfavorable variances.
- The outside firm may not fully understand the manufacturing process; this could result in poor management decisions based on faulty information.

(CMA)

63. a. The major advantages of using a standard cost accounting system include the following:
- Budgeting. Standard costs can be the building blocks for budget preparation and allow the development of flexible budgeting.
- Performance evaluation. By comparing actual costs to standard costs, the performance of the company, department, activity center, or individual can be evaluated.
- Controlling. An analysis of the variances between actual and standard costs can identify the problem areas and allow for remedial action.
- Pricing. Standard costs based on normal activity levels may form an acceptable basis for pricing strategies that provide for full recovery of all costs.
- Recordkeeping. Standard costs reduce the effort required to perform cost accounting and, thus, reduce the cost of bookkeeping.

b. The setting of physical standards such as material quantities, labor hours, machine time, and setup time generally requires information about material specifications and work flow; this information is generated from studies conducted by technical personnel or from the production expertise of line personnel. There must be adequate cost and price information to convert the physical standards into monetary terms. In addition, a firm's cost must be separable into cost per unit of production or hour of service, and the production process must be fairly stable and predictable.

c. 1. Because cash maximization is important for a product classified as a cash cow, efficiency of operations is essential. Standard costing will provide targets for monitoring costs and identification of inefficiencies so that they can be corrected. Because a cash cow is a slow-growing, established product, costs should be fairly predictable and easy to track.

2.   Because a product classified as a question mark is facing strong competition, the ability to control product costs may be the difference between success and failure. The efficiency gained from the application and monitoring of a standard cost system could give the question mark a longer time to gain market acceptance. The cost control afforded by standard costing might permit a firm to be more flexible in its pricing, including the ability to price its question marks below similar competitive products.

(CMA)

Ethics and Quality Discussions

65. a.   The customers risk loss of competitive advantage. For example, the vendor representative of a particular supplier could provide critical information to competitors. The firms also risk loss of capability to provide for their own purchases. Becoming dependent on a supplier for purchasing activities makes it very difficult to change suppliers should the firm need or want to do so.

b.   Many costs associated with the purchasing function would be saved. For example, phone calls to suppliers and the cost of issuing purchase orders could be avoided. Additionally, costs could be saved on inventory storage, handling received parts and materials, obsolescence, and quality inspection.

c.   The purchase price variance would virtually disappear as a managerial concern. Presumably purchase prices would be agreed to in long-term contracts and any deviation from such prices would be a matter for negotiation between management of the two firms.

d.   The implementation of JIT II might reduce material quantity standards because the quality of material would be constant and provide for fewer defective items; thus, the standard could be reduced for a waste minimization factor. Labor time standards might also be reduced because the vendors might call for more standard parts to be used, which would minimize changeover time; additionally, the reduction in defects would reduce the time for rework or the built-in margin for error.

e.   The implementation of JIT II would probably cause product quality to increase. The on-site suppliers would want to make certain that the best possible product was being produced from the materials being supplied. Therefore, they would probably be called on to help investigate variances and to provide suggestions for methods of improvement. Delivery of low grade material would destroy the underlying foundation of trust in the JIT II system.

67.   a.   It is indeterminate. In some cases, because of
           governmental support programs, wages paid directly by the
           company to the disabled may be less than to nondisabled
           persons. Such a situation is perfectly ethical; however,
           paying the disabled lower wages simply because they will
           accept less is not ethical.

           As to time standards, a disabled person may take
           longer than a nondisabled person to perform certain
           tasks. Sometimes, however, disabled persons may function
           better than the average nondisabled person--either
           because their disability is unrelated to their job
           performance (such as sitting in a wheelchair versus
           sitting in a chair), because their disability actually
           benefits their performance (such as a hearing-impaired
           factory worker not being distracted by loud noises), or
           perhaps because they have fewer options or because they
           have had to learn to deal better with adversity (such as
           a blind typist transcribing tapes on a word processor).

      b.   Perhaps the disabled person may be given a longer
           training or trial employment period to efficiently learn
           the task because of any initial difficulties of
           adjusting. Special physical adjustments (such as lowering
           controls or making certain that ramps are available) may
           also be needed; if these are neither available or nor
           easily accessible, performance may not be what it could
           be and consideration should be given to such matters.

           Supervisors should, however, not condone behavior by
           the disabled worker that would cause reprimands to the
           nondisabled. Such a situation will create friction among
           the workers and constitute unfair and unethical treatment
           of the nondisabled.

      c.   Issues to consider: societal effect of having the
           disabled work at jobs that they can perform rather than
           being on governmental aid; societal effect of possibly
           having nondisabled persons out of work; potentially
           higher costs of products because of putting in special
           equipment or access; the rights of all people to have the
           ability to earn a basic living (are these being violated
           in part by having preference systems?).

      d.   Each student will have a different answer to this
           question. Students should, however, recognize that
           "diversity" pertains to all differences among people--not
           simply the most commonly referred to ones of race or
           religion.

e. Roberts should make his decision based on whether Sima can effectively and efficiently do the job, given a reasonable learning period and the proper accessibility of equipment. A comparison of Sima's previous accomplishment and job-related physical abilities with those of the other candidates should give an indication of his abilities. Finally, Flower Mound Corp. must abide by the guidelines of Americans with Disabilities Act.

69. a. Each student will have a different answer to this question.

b. Paying someone less than a living wage is unethical. Students may want to debate, however, the issue that $.20 per hour is a living wage in Vietnam. Such a discussion should lead to whether a $.20 per hour wage will ever help advance a Third World country out of a cycle of poverty.

c. Each student will have a different answer to this question. However, with age comes experience and setting an "adult-based" time standard for children is unethical.

Chapter 9
Introduction to a Standard Cost System

CHAPTER 10
PROCESS COSTING

Questions

1. A company that produces homogeneous goods in mass quantities is likely to use a process costing system. The company can either have a single department or multiple departments.

3. Yes, a company can use both job order and process costing for its production activities--but not for the same types of activities. For example, a bakery could use process costing for its daily production of breads or cookies, but could use job order costing for wedding cakes. A barbecue restaurant could use process costing for its regular barbecue, but could use job order costing for a catered event. A clothes manufacturer could use process costing for mass-produced, "off-the-rack" clothes, but could use job order costing for custom designed clothes.

5. It is appropriate to apply actual overhead cost to products in a process costing environment if both actual overhead and production volume are relatively constant each period.

7. No. Typically, material, labor and overhead are added at different times or rates in a production process. If products are at different stages of completion with regard to each cost category, then a separate equivalent unit computation is necessary for each cost pool.

9. The two methods of process costing are weighted average and FIFO. Both methods use the concept of equivalent units of production to assign costs to output. Both methods treat all current period work (started and completed as well as ending inventory) in the same manner. Both develop an average cost of production for each distinctive cost component.
    The weighted average method does not distinguish between work performed in prior periods on the current period's beginning inventory from work performed in the current period on the beginning inventory. Alternatively, FIFO separately accounts for the work performed on and the costs of beginning inventory. These costs are not commingled with current-period work or costs. Thus, the result is a difference in the quantity of EUP calculated and the cost per EUP.

11. Total production costs are assigned to the goods that (a) have
     been completed and transferred to the successor department or
     to finished goods inventory and (b) are not yet finished by
     the department. At the end of the period, the costs of the
     units in the first group will appear in the WIP account of the
     successor department (if not yet completed), in finished goods
     inventory, or in cost of goods sold. At the end of the period,
     the costs of the units in the latter group will appear in the
     WIP inventory of the department in which they reside.

13. Transferred out cost refers to departmental costs that have
     been assigned to goods that have been completed by the
     department and transferred either to a successor WIP
     department or to Finished Goods Inventory.
          Under the FIFO method, the computation for goods
     transferred out involves two elements: one relates to those
     units in beginning inventory and the other to those units that
     were started and completed in the current period. Each of
     these groups of units will likely have different costs for
     each of the cost components. The current period costs to
     complete the beginning inventory are added to the costs
     previously incurred for the beginning inventory costs. The
     units started and completed in the current period are costed
     entirely at current period costs. Such a distinction is not
     required under the weighted average method because beginning
     inventory and current period costs are commingled.

15. The equation is: BI + TP = EI + TO

17. FIFO provides the better picture because it isolates the work
     performed (and the costs incurred) in the current period from
     the work performed in prior periods on units in the department
     at the beginning of a period. The weighted average method
     commingles work performed in the prior period on beginning
     inventory and work performed in the current period.

19. FIFO would assign a higher cost to the ending work in process.
     Under FIFO, the cost per EUP is based on only the current
     period's costs (which would, in an inflationary environment,
     be higher than those of the prior period). Alternatively,
     weighted average would assign a cost to ending WIP based on an
     average of the prior (lower) and current period costs.

21. If a department is not the first department in a sequential
     process, it will have a cost component called *Transferred In*.
     This cost component represents the cost of all predecessor
     departments for the goods transferred into a department during
     a period. All the units in this component will be 100%
     complete as to the prior departments.

23. Spoilage creates an important cost of quality. As such, spoilage costs should be monitored so that a formal evaluation can be made of efforts to control spoilage costs. If not specifically tracked, spoilage costs are merely averaged over the good units produced. In tracking spoilage costs, some firms may want to distinguish between expected (or normal) spoilage and unexpected (abnormal) spoilage. World-class companies, however, would generally utilize a zero defects concept that would classify all spoilage as abnormal.

25. The cost of spoilage is difficult to determine for a service provider because spoilage is often defined as "poor service." If a customer does not complain and simply does not return to use the services of the provider again, there is no way to determine the cost impact on the company.

27. The journal entry would be a debit to Work in Process Inventory-Cutting and a credit to Work in Process Inventory-Cleaning for $20,000.

Exercises

29. a. Total pounds to account for = 32,000 + 800,000 = <u>832,000</u>

    b.
Beginning inventory (32,000 × 100%)	32,000
Started and completed [(808,000 - 32,000) × 100%]	776,000
Ending inventory [(832,000 - 808,000) × 100%]	<u>24,000</u>
Total EUP for direct material	<u>832,000</u>

    c.
Beginning inventory (32,000 × 100%)	32,000
Started and completed [776,000 × 100%]	776,000
Ending inventory [(832,000 - 808,000) × 35%]	<u>8,400</u>
Total EUP for conversion	<u>816,400</u>

31. a. Total pounds to account for = 32,000 + 800,000 = <u>832,000</u>

    b.
Beginning inventory (32,000 × 0%)	0
Started and completed [(808,000 - 32,000) × 100%]	776,000
Ending inventory [(832,000 - 808,000) × 100%]	<u>24,000</u>
Total EUP for direct material	<u>800,000</u>

    c.
Beginning inventory (32,000 × 40%)	12,800
Started and completed [776,000 × 100%]	776,000
Ending inventory [24,000 × 35%]	<u>8,400</u>
Total EUP for conversion	<u>797,200</u>

33. a.   Beginning inventory (40,000 × 100%)   40,000
           Started and completed [(200,000 - 40,000) × 100%] 160,000
           Ending inventory (120,000 × 75%)   90,000
           Total EUP   290,000

     b.   Units transferred out = BI + Started - EI = 40,000 +
              240,000 - 60,000 = 220,000

           Beginning inventory (40,000 × 100%)   40,000
           Started and completed [(220,000 - 40,000) × 100%] 180,000
           Ending inventory (60,000 × 60%)   36,000
           Total EUP   256,000

     c.   Ending inventory = BI + Started - Transferred = 15,000 +
              135,000 - 130,000 = 20,000

           Beginning inventory (15,000 × 100%)   15,000
           Started and completed [(130,000 - 15,000) × 100%] 115,000
           Ending inventory (20,000 × 90%)   18,000
           Total EUP   148,000

     d.   Units started = Transferred + EI - BI = 180,000 + 20,000
              - 10,000 = 190,000

           Beginning inventory (10,000 × 100%)   10,000
           Started and completed [(180,000 - 10,000) × 100%] 170,000
           Ending inventory (20,000 × 70%)   14,000
           Total EUP   194,000

35. a.   Ending inventory = (70,000 + 360,000 - 395,000) = 35,000

	DM	CONVERSION
Beginning inventory	70,000	70,000
S&C (395,000 - 70,000)	325,000	325,000
EI (80%; 45%)	28,000	15,750
Total EUP	423,000	410,750

     b.

	DM	CONVERSION
Beginning inventory (10%; 40%)	7,000	28,000
S&C (395,000 - 70,000)	325,000	325,000
EI (80%; 45%)	28,000	15,750
Total EUP	360,000	368,750

     c.

	DM	CONVERSION
EUP under WA	423,000	410,750
Work performed on BI in prior period	(63,000)	(42,000)
EUP under FIFO	360,000	368,750

37. a.

	DM	CONVERSION
Beginning inventory	42,000	42,000
S&C (150,000 - 42,000)	108,000	108,000
EI (100%; 60%)	30,000	18,000
Total EUP	180,000	168,000

b.

	DM	CONVERSION
Beginning inventory cost	$ 6,420	$ 7,056
Current cost	15,180	34,944
Total cost	$ 21,600	$ 42,000
Divided by EUP	180,000	168,000
Cost per EUP	$.12	$.25

c. Transferred out = 150,000 × $.37 = $55,500
Ending inventory:

Direct material (30,000 × $.12)	$3,600
Conversion (30,000 × 60% × $.25)	4,500
Cost of ending inventory	$8,100

39. a.

	DM	CONVERSION
Beginning inventory (0%; 25%)	0	10,500
S&C (150,000 - 42,000)	108,000	108,000
Ending inventory (100%; 60%)	30,000	18,000
Total EUP	138,000	136,500

b.

	DM	CONVERSION
Current cost	$ 15,180	$ 34,944
Divided by EUP	138,000	136,500
Cost per EUP	$.11	$.256

c. Transferred out:

Beginning inventory cost	$13,476	
Cost to complete (10,500 × $.256)	2,688	
Started & completed (108,000 × $.366)	39,528	$55,692
Ending inventory:		
Direct material (30,000 × $.11)	$ 3,300	
Conversion (30,000 × 60% × $.256)	4,608	$ 7,908

41. a. Started & completed = Started - EI = 120,000 - 12,000
= 108,000 quarts

	DM	CONVERSION
Beginning inventory (0%; 70%)	0	21,000
Started and completed	108,000	108,000
Ending inventory (100%; 80%)	12,000	9,600
Total EUP	120,000	138,600

b. Cost of goods completed (138,000 × $2.60) = $358,800

Cost of ending inventory:

Direct material (12,000 × $1.20)	$14,400
Conversion [9,600 × ($.85 + $.55)]	13,440
Total cost of ending inventory	$27,840

43. a.   Started & completed = Transferred in - EI = 80,000 - 30,000 = 50,000 calendars

	TI	DM	CONVERSION
BI (100%; 0%; 30%)	20,000	0	6,000
Started and completed	50,000	50,000	50,000
EI (100%; 0%; 80%)	30,000	0	24,000
Total EUP	100,000	70,000	94,000

     b.

	TI	DM	CONVERSION
BI cost	$ 25,000	$ 0	$ 1,114
Current costs	80,000	10,500	14,960
Total cost	$105,000	$10,500	$16,074
Divided by EUP	100,000	70,000	94,000
Cost per EUP	$1.05	$.15	$.171

     c.   Cost transferred to Finished Goods Inventory = ($70,000 × $1.371) = <u>$95,970</u>

     d.   Cost of ending inventory:

Transferred in (30,000 × $1.05)	$31,500
Direct material (30,000 × 0% × $.15)	0
Conversion (30,000 × 80% × $.171)	4,104
Total cost of ending inventory	$35,604

45. a.   Started & completed = Transferred in - EI = 80,000 - 30,000 = 50,000 calendars

	TI	DM	CONVERSION
BI (0%; 100%; 70%)	0	20,000	14,000
Started and completed	50,000	50,000	50,000
EI (100%; 0%; 80%)	30,000	0	24,000
Total EUP	80,000	70,000	88,000

     b.

	TI	DM	CONVERSION
Current costs	$80,000	$10,500	$14,960
Divided by EUP	80,000	70,000	88,000
Cost per EUP	$1.00	$.15	$.17

     c.   Cost transferred to Finished Goods Inventory:

Cost of BI ($25,000 + $1,114)	$26,114
Cost to complete:	
Direct material (20,000 × $.15)	3,000
Conversion (14,000 × $.17)	2,380
S&C [50,000 × ($1.00 + $.15 + $.17)]	66,000
Total cost transferred	$97,494

     d.   Cost of ending inventory:

Transferred in (30,000 × $1.00)	$30,000
Direct material (30,000 × 0% × $.15)	0
Conversion (30,000 × 60% × $.17)	4,080
Total cost of ending inventory	$34,080

47. a. Work in Process Inventory-Dehydration 200,000
       Raw Material Inventory   200,000

    b. Work in Process Inventory-Dehydration 160,000
        Overhead-Dehydration   80,000
           Wages Payable   240,000

    c. Overhead-Dehydration   140,000
        Various accounts   140,000

    d. Work in Process Inventory-Pelletizing 660,000
        Work in Process Inventory-Dehydration   660,000

    e. Work in Process Inventory-Pelletizing 124,000
        Overhead-Pelletizing   38,000
           Wages Payable   162,000

    f. Overhead-Pelletizing   226,000
        Various accounts   226,000

    g. Finished Goods Inventory   980,000
        Work in Process-Pelletizing   980,000

    h. Cost of Goods Sold   900,000
        Finished Goods Inventory   900,000
       Cash   1,460,000
        Sales   1,460,000

Problems

49.
Cost of Production Report
(Weighted Average Method)

PRODUCTION DATA	WHOLE UNITS	EQUIVALENT UNITS OF PRODUCTION DM	CONVERSION
BI (100%; 40%)	12,000	12,000	4,800
Tons started	90,000		
To account for	102,000		
BI completed	12,000	0	7,200
S&C	80,000	80,000	80,000
Tons completed	92,000		
EI (100%; 30%)	10,000	10,000	3,000
Accounted for	102,000	102,000	95,000

COST DATA

	TOTAL	DM	CONVERSION
BI cost	$ 133,590	$ 82,980	$ 50,610
Current costs	1,527,490	630,000	897,490
Total cost to account for	$1,661,080	$712,980	$948,100
Divided by EUP		102,000	95,000
Cost per EUP	$16.97	$6.99	$9.98

COST ASSIGNMENT

Transferred out (92,000 × $16.97)		$1,561,240
Ending inventory:		
Direct material (10,000 × $6.99)	$69,900	
Conversion (3,000 × $9.98)	29,940	99,840
Total cost accounted for		$1,661,080

51.
Cost of Production Report
(FIFO Method)

PRODUCTION DATA	WHOLE UNITS	EQUIVALENT UNITS OF PRODUCTION DM	CONVERSION
BI (100%; 40%)	12,000	12,000	4,800
Tons started	90,000		
To account for	102,000		
BI completed	12,000	0	7,200
S&C	80,000	80,000	80,000
Tons completed	92,000		
EI (100%; 30%)	10,000	10,000	3,000
Accounted for	102,000	90,000	90,200

COST DATA

	TOTAL	DM	CONVERSION
BI cost	$ 133,590		
Current costs	1,527,490	$630,000	$897,490
Total cost to account for	$1,661,080		
Divided by EUP		90,000	90,200
Cost per EUP	$16.95	$7.00	$9.95

COST ASSIGNMENT

Transferred out:		
BI costs	$ 133,590	
Cost to complete:		
Conversion (7,200 × $9.95)	71,640	
Total cost of BI transferred	$ 205,230	
S&C (80,000 × $16.95)	1,356,000	$1,561,230
Ending inventory:		
Direct material (10,000 × $7.00)	$ 70,000	
Conversion (3,000 × $9.95)	29,850	99,850
Total cost accounted for		$1,661,080

53. a. Total units to account for = 20,000 + 100,000 = 120,000

b. Number of units S&C = 100,000 - 25,000 = 75,000

c. Total cost to account for = $785 + $915 + $15,190 + $8,400 = $25,290

d.

	DM	CONVERSION
Beginning inventory (100%)	20,000	20,000
Started and completed	75,000	75,000
Ending inventory (70%; 80%)	17,500	20,000
Total EUP	112,500	115,000

e.

	DM	CONVERSION
Beginning inventory cost	$ 785	$ 915
Current cost	15,190	8,400
Total cost	$15,975	$ 9,315
Divided by EUP	112,500	115,000
Cost per EUP	$.142	$.081

f. Transferred out = 95,000 × $.223 = $21,185

Ending inventory:	
Direct material (17,500 × $.142)	$2,485
Conversion (20,000 × $.081)	1,620
Cost of ending inventory	$4,105

g.

	DM	CONVERSION
Beginning inventory (80%; 50%)	16,000	10,000
Started and completed	75,000	75,000
Ending inventory (70%; 80%)	17,500	20,000
Total EUP	108,500	105,000

h.

	DM	CONVERSION
Current cost	$15,190	$ 8,400
Divided by EUP	108,500	105,000
Cost per EUP	$.14	$.08

i. Transferred out:
    Beginning inventory cost $ 1,700
    Cost to complete
        Material (16,000 × $.14)   2,240
        Conversion (10,000 × $.08)   800
    Started & completed (75,000 × $.22) 16,500 $21,240
    Ending inventory:
        Direct material (17,500 × $.14) $ 2,450
        Conversion (20,000 × $.08)   1,600 $ 4,050

55. a. Started & completed = 97,000 - 12,000 = 85,000

	DAIRY	PECANS	CONVERSION
BI (100%)	12,000	12,000	12,000
S&C	85,000	85,000	85,000
EI (100%; 60%; 70%)	5,000	0	4,000
Total EUP	102,000	97,000	101,000

b.

	DAIRY	PECANS	CONVERSION
Total cost	$107,100	$29,100	$88,880
Divided by EUP	102,000	97,000	101,000
Cost per EUP	$1.05	$.30	$.88

c. Transferred out = 97,000 × $2.23 = $216,310
    Ending inventory:
       Dairy (5,000 × $1.05) $5,250
       Conversion (4,000 × $.88)   3,520
       Cost of ending inventory $8,770

d.

	DAIRY	PECANS	CONVERSION
Total cost	$107,100	$29,100	$88,880
Divided by EUP	96,000	91,000	95,000
Cost per EUP	$1.12	$.32	$.94

The cost of spoilage is the higher cost per gallon of ice cream multiplied by the number of spoiled gallons or ($2.38 × 6,000) = $14,280.

57.   Cost of Production Report-Machining
        (Weighted Average Method)

PRODUCTION DATA · EQUIVALENT UNITS OF PRODUCTION

	WHOLE UNITS	DM	CONVERSION
BI (100%; 40%)	500*	500	200
Units started	40,000		
To account for	40,500		
BI completed	500	0	300
S&C	38,000	38,000	38,000
Units completed	38,500		
EI	2,000**	2,000	1,600
Accounted for	40,500	40,500	40,100

COST DATA

	TOTAL	DM	CONVERSION
BI cost	$ 16,245	$ 11,140	$ 5,105
Current costs	1,412,450	794,000	618,450
Total cost to account for	$1,428,695	$805,140	$623,555
Divided by EUP		40,500	40,100
Cost per EUP	$35.43	$19.88	$15.55

COST ASSIGNMENT

Transferred out (38,500 × $35.43)		$1,364,055
Ending inventory:		
Direct material (2,000 × $19.88)	$39,760	
Conversion (1,600 × $15.55)	24,880	64,640
Total cost accounted for		$1,428,695

*Fully complete as to direct material; 40% as to conversion.
**Fully complete as to direct material; 80% as to conversion.

Cost of Production Report-Finishing
(Weighted Average Method)

PRODUCTION DATA · EQUIVALENT UNITS OF PRODUCTION

	WHOLE UNITS	TRANSFERRED IN	DM	CONVERSION
BI	350*	350	0	105
Units TI	38,500			
To account for	38,850			
BI completed	350	0	350	245
S&C	37,900	37,900	37,900	37,900
Units completed	38,250			
EI	600**	600	0	360
Accounted for	38,850	38,850	38,250	38,610

COST DATA

	TOTAL	TRANSFERRED IN	DM	CONVERSION
BI cost	$ 15,768	$ 11,235	$ 0	$ 4,533
Current costs	1,743,362	1,364,055	133,875	246,432
Total cost to account for	$1,760,130	$1,375,290	$133,875	$250,965
Divided by EUP		38,850	38,250	38,610
Cost per EUP	$45.40	$35.40	$3.50	$6.50

COST ASSIGNMENT

Transferred out (38,250 × $45.40)		$1,736,550
Ending inventory:		
Transferred in (600 × $35.40)	$21,240	
Conversion (360 × $6.50)	2,340	23,580
Total cost accounted for		$1,760,130

*Fully complete as to transferred-in; 0% as to direct material; 30% as to conversion.
**Fully complete as to transferred-in; 0% as to direct material; 60% as to conversion.

59.   Cost of Production Report-Machining
                            (FIFO Method)

PRODUCTION DATA   **EQUIVALENT UNITS OF PRODUCTION**

	WHOLE UNITS	DM	CONVERSION
BI (100%; 40%)	500*	500	200
Units started	40,000		
To account for	40,500		
BI completed	500	0	300
S&C	38,000	38,000	38,000
Units completed	38,500		
EI	2,000**	2,000	1,600
Accounted for	40,500	40,000	39,900

COST DATA

	TOTAL	DM	CONVERSION
BI cost	$ 16,245		
Current costs	1,412,450	$794,000	$618,450
Total cost to account for	$1,428,695		
Divided by EUP		40,000	39,900
Cost per EUP	$35.35	$19.85	$15.50

COST ASSIGNMENT

Transferred out:		
Beginning inventory cost	$ 16,245	
Cost to complete		
Conversion (300 × $15.50)	4,650	
S&C (38,000 × $35.35)	1,343,300	$1,364,195
Ending inventory:		
DM (2,000 × $19.85)	$ 39,700	
Conversion (1,600 × $15.50)	24,800	64,500
Total cost accounted for		$1,428,695

Cost of Production Report-Finishing
(FIFO Method)

PRODUCTION DATA

EQUIVALENT UNITS OF PRODUCTION

	WHOLE UNITS	TRANSFERRED IN	DM	CONVERSION
BI	350*	350	0	105
Units TI	38,500			
To account for	38,850			
BI completed	350	0	350	245
S&C	37,900	37,900	37,900	37,900
Units completed	38,250			
EI	600**	600	0	360
Accounted for	38,850	38,500	38,250	38,505

COST DATA

	TOTAL	TRANSFERRED IN	DM	CONVERSION
BI cost	$ 15,768			
Current costs	1,743,362	$1,364,055	$133,875	$246,432
Total cost to account for	$1,760,130			
Divided by EUP		38,500	38,250	38,505
Cost per EUP	$45.33	$35.43	$3.50	$6.40

COST ASSIGNMENT

Transferred out:		
Beginning inventory cost	$ 15,768	
Cost to complete		
Direct material (350 × $3.50)	1,225	
Conversion (245 × $6.40)	1,568	
S&C (37,900 × $45.33)	1,718,007	$1,736,568
Ending inventory:		
TI (600 × $35.43)	$ 21,258	
Conversion (360 × $6.40)	2,304	23,562
Total cost accounted for		$1,760,130

61. a.   Cost of Production Report
                        (Weighted Average Method)

PRODUCTION DATA   **EQUIVALENT UNITS OF PRODUCTION**

	WHOLE UNITS	MAT. A	MAT. B	DL	OH
BI	10,000*	10,000	0	4,000	6,000
Units TI	80,000				
To account for	90,000				
BI completed	10,000	0	10,000	6,000	4,000
S&C	65,000	65,000	65,000	65,000	65,000
Units completed	75,000				
EI	15,000**	15,000	0	4,500	6,000
Accounted for	90,000	90,000	75,000	79,500	81,000

COST DATA

	TOTAL	MAT. A	MAT. B	DL	OH
BI cost	$ 4,625	$1,900	$ 0	$1,195	$ 1,530
Current costs	62,050	8,000	37,500	7,550	9,000
Total cost to account for	$66,675	$9,900	$37,500	$8,745	$10,530
Divided by EUP		90,000	75,000	79,500	81,000
Cost per EUP	$.85	$.11	$.50	$.11	$.13

COST ASSIGNMENT

Transferred out (75,000 × $.85)		$63,750
Ending inventory:		
Material A (15,000 × $.11)	$1,650	
Direct labor (4,500 × $.11)	495	
Overhead (6,000 × $.13)	780	2,925
Total cost accounted for		$66,675

*Fully complete as to material A; 0% as to material B; 40% as to labor; 60% as to overhead.
** Fully complete as to material A; 0% as to material B; 30% as to labor; 40% as to overhead.

b. Cost of Production Report
(FIFO Method)

PRODUCTION DATA / EQUIVALENT UNITS OF PRODUCTION

	WHOLE UNITS	MAT. A	MAT. B	DL	OH
BI	10,000*	10,000	0	4,000	6,000
Units TI	80,000				
To account for	90,000				
BI completed	10,000	0	10,000	6,000	4,000
S&C	65,000	65,000	65,000	65,000	65,000
Units completed	75,000				
EI	15,000**	15,000	0	4,500	6,000
Accounted for	90,000	80,000	75,000	75,500	75,000

COST DATA

	TOTAL	MAT. A	MAT. B	DL	OH
BI cost	$ 4,625				
Current costs	62,050	$8,000	$37,500	$7,550	$9,000
Total cost to account for	$66,675				
Divided by EUP		80,000	75,000	75,500	75,000
Cost per EUP	$.82	$.10	$.50	$.10	$.12

COST ASSIGNMENT

Transferred out:		
Beginning inventory cost	$ 4,625	
Cost to complete		
Material B (10,000 × $.50)	5,000	
Direct labor (6,000 × $.10)	600	
Overhead (4,000 × $.12)	480	
Total cost of BI	$10,705	
S&C (65,000 × $.82)	53,300	$64,005
Ending inventory:		
Material A (15,000 × $.10)	$ 1,500	
Direct labor (4,500 × $.10)	450	
Overhead (6,000 × $.12)	720	2,670
Total cost accounted for		$66,675

*Fully complete as to material A; 0% as to material B; 40% as to labor; 60% as to overhead.
** Fully complete as to material A; 0% as to material B; 30% as to labor; 40% as to overhead.

c. The weighted average method disguises poor cost control by commingling the beginning inventory costs and units with costs of and units produced in the current period. This commingling eliminates any opportunity to observe distinct cost differences between periods.

63. a.   ASSEMBLY

	WHOLE UNITS	DM	CONVERSION
BI (100%; 50%)	10,000	10,000	5,000
Units started	20,000		
To account for	30,000		
BI completed	10,000	0	5,000
S&C	16,000	16,000	16,000
Units completed	26,000		
EI (100%; 40%)	4,000	4,000	1,600
Accounted for	30,000	20,000	22,600

COST DATA

	TOTAL	DM	CONVERSION
BI cost	$14,300		
Current costs	34,204	$22,000	$12,204
Total cost to account for	$48,504		
Divided by EUP		20,000	22,600
Cost per EUP	$1.64	$1.10	$.54

                                    FINISHING

	WHOLE UNITS	TRANSFERRED IN	DM	CONVERSION
BI	12,000*	12,000	0	9,000
Units TI	26,000			
To account for	38,000			
BI completed	12,000	0	12,000	3,000
S&C	16,000	16,000	16,000	16,000
Units completed	28,000			
EI	10,000**	10,000	0	2,500
Accounted for	38,000	38,000	28,000	30,500

COST DATA

	TOTAL	TRANSFERRED IN	DM	CONVERSION
BI cost	$23,960	$17,560	$ 0	$ 6,400
Current costs	75,240	43,240	14,000	18,000
Total cost to account for	$99,200	$60,800	$14,000	$24,400
Divided by EUP		38,000	28,000	20,500
Cost per EUP	$2.90	$1.60	$.50	$.80

COST ASSIGNMENT

Transferred out (28,000 × $2.90)		$81,200
Ending inventory:		
Transferred in (10,000 × $1.60)	$16,000	
Conversion (2,500 × $.80)	2,000	18,000
Total cost accounted for		$99,200

*Fully complete as to transferred in; 0% as to direct material; 75% as to conversion.
**Fully complete as to transferred in; 0% as to direct material; 25% as to conversion.

b.

Work in Process-Assembly	34,204	
Raw Material Inventory		22,000
Wages Payable		8,136
Various accounts (for overhead)		4,068
Work in Process-Finishing	43,240	
Work in Process-Assembly		43,240
Work in Process-Finishing	32,000	
Raw Material Inventory		14,000
Wages Payable		9,000
Various accounts (for overhead)		9,000
Finished Goods Inventory	81,200	
Work in Process-Finishing		81,200
Cost of Goods Sold	81,200	
Finished Goods Inventory		81,200
Cash	162,400	
Sales Revenue		162,400

Cases

65. a.

	EXTRUSION	FORM	TRIM	FINISH
Material costs	$192,000	$ 44,000	$15,000	$12,000
÷ Units produced	16,000	11,000	5,000	2,000
Unit cost	$12.00	$4.00	$3.00	$6.00
Conversion costs	$392,000	$132,000	$69,000	$42,000
÷ Units produced	16,000	11,000	5,000	2,000
Unit cost	$24.50	$12.00	$13.80	$21.00

UNIT COSTS

	PLASTIC SHEETS	STANDARD MODEL	DELUXE MODEL	EXECUTIVE MODEL
Extrusion mat.	$12.00	$12.00	$12.00	$12.00
Form mat.	-	4.00	4.00	4.00
Trim mat.	-	-	3.00	3.00
Finish mat.	-	-	-	6.00
Extrusion conv.	24.50	24.50	24.50	24.50
Form conv.	-	12.00	12.00	12.00
Trim conv.	-	-	13.80	13.80
Finish conv.	-	-	-	21.00
Total unit cost	$36.50	$52.50	$69.30	$96.30
Units produced	× 5,000	× 6,000	× 3,000	× 2,000
Total cost	$182,500	$315,000	$207,900	$192,600

b.

EQUIVALENT UNITS

Entering trim operation:	MATERIAL %	Qty.	CONVERSION %	Qty.
2,000 Deluxe units	100	2,000	100	2,000
1,000 Deluxe units	100	1,000	60	600
2,000 Executive units	100	2,000	100	2,000
Total equivalent units		5,000		4,600

Deluxe model WIP costs:	UNIT COST	TOTAL COST
Extrusion material	$12.00	$12,000
Form material	4.00	4,000
Trim material (100%)	3.00	3,000
Extrusion conversion	24.50	24,500
Form conversion	12.00	12,000
Trim conversion (60%)	9.00*	9,000*
Total work-in-process costs	$64.50	$64,500

*Conversion cost = ($30,000 + $39,000) ÷ 4,600 = $15 per equivalent unit.

(CMA)

67. a.

	WHOLE UNITS	WRAP	BOXES	DL	OH
BI	10,000*	10,000	0	4,000	4,000
Units TI	40,000				
To account for	50,000				
BI completed	10,000	0	10,000	6,000	6,000
S&C	30,000	30,000	30,000	30,000	30,000
Units completed	40,000				
EI	10,000**	10,000	10,000	8,000	8,000
Accounted for	50,000	40,000	50,000	44,000	44,000

*Fully complete as to wrap; 0% as to boxes; 40% as to labor and overhead.
**Fully complete as to wrap and boxes; 80% as to labor and overhead.

b.

	TOTAL	WRAP	BOXES	DL	OH
Current costs	$218,000	$80,000	$50,000	$22,000	$66,000
Divided by EUP		40,000	50,000	44,000	44,000
Cost per EUP	$5.00	$2.00	$1.00	$.50	$1.50

c. If $5,000 is considered an immaterial amount for Shine-Brite Company, the additional overhead incurred would be charged to Cost of Goods Sold for October. If $5,000 is material, the underapplied overhead should be prorated among Cost of Goods Sold, Finished Goods Inventory, and Work in Process Inventory.

(CMA)

Ethics and Quality Discussions

69. Each student will have a different answer to this question. No solution provided.

71. a. The increase in minimum wage could positively affect quality in two ways. First, the least productive and effective employees could be dismissed in response to the increase. These employees could be responsible for existing quality problems. Second, to avoid paying the higher wages, some firms may opt to acquire new technology that requires less labor to operate. Such technology could result in improved quality.

Alternatively, quality could be adversely affected if firms try to do the same amount of work with fewer workers. Employees may become more stressed and overwhelmed with their expanded responsibilities. This situation could lead to reductions in the quality level of output.

b.   Ethically, managers have a responsibility to deal
     honestly with employees as the managers respond to the
     increase in the minimum wage. One of the biggest
     challenges will be in low-pay industries. In these
     industries, as the lowest paid workers receive an
     increase in their pay rate, there may be compression in
     the wage rates across workers. After the minimum wage
     increase, there will be less difference in pay between
     the highest and lowest paid workers. This compression
     will create a demand to adjust the pay of workers who
     were not directly affected by the minimum wage increase.
     If the industry is not profitable enough to allow such
     increases, workers at the higher end of the pay scale
     will perceive that they are not being treated fairly.
     Thus, it is necessary for the management to maintain a
     perception of fairness in the wages paid to the various
     workers.

          If layoffs are necessary because of the increased
     labor bill, management must be equitable in determining
     which workers to terminate. A valid basis such as job
     tenure and/or productivity should be used as criteria to
     determine which workers are to be maintained.

73. a.   Each student will have a different answer to this
          question.

     b.   Each student will have a different answer to this
          question.

     c.   Employee empowerment in a process environment should:
          reduce direct labor time and therefore cost; move direct
          labor to a more indirect category and, thus, create
          additional indirect labor overhead; decrease spoilage;
          and speed up the production process.

75. a.   George Wilson's considerations are determined largely by
          his position as cost accountant, with responsibilities to
          FulRange, Inc. others in the company, and himself.
          Wilson's job involves collecting, analyzing, and
          reporting operating information. Although not responsible
          for product quality, Wilson should exercise initiative
          and good judgment in proving management with information
          having potential adverse economic impact.

               Wilson should determine whether the controller's
          request violates his professional or personal standards,
          or the company's code of ethics. As Wilson decides how to
          proceed, he should protect proprietary information he has
          and should not violate the chain of command by discussing
          this matter with the controller's superiors.

b. 1. The controller has reporting responsibilities and should protect overall company interests by encouraging his staff to further study the problem, by informing his superiors in this matter, and by working with other employees to find solutions.

2. The quality control engineer has a responsibility for product quality and should protect the overall company interests by continuing to study the quality of reworked rejects, informing the plant managers and his staff in this matter, and working with others in the company to find solutions.

3. The plant manager and his staff are responsible for product quality and cost and should protect the company interests by exercising appropriate stewardship and ensuring that products meet the quality standards. Absentee owners need information from management, and the plant manager and his staff have a responsibility to inform the board of directors elected by the owners of any problems that could affect the well-being of FulRange.

c. George Wilson needs to protect the interests of FulRange, others in the company, and himself. Wilson is vulnerable if he conceals the problem and it eventually surfaces. Wilson must take some action to reduce his vulnerability. One possible action that Wilson could take would be to obey the controller and prepare the advance material for the board without mentioning or highlighting the probable failure of reworks. Because this differs from his long-standing practice of highlighting information with potential adverse economic impact, Wilson should write a report to the controller detailing the probable failure of reworks, the analysis made by himself and the quality control engineer, and the controller's instructions in this matter.

(CMA)

Chapter 10
Process Costing

CHAPTER 11
CONTROLLING INVENTORY AND PRODUCTION COSTS

Questions

1. A items are those having the highest dollar volume; these are likely to be some of the most expensive parts and materials used in production. C items are those having the lowest dollar volume; these are likely to be parts and materials that are used in small volume or are of very low value on a per unit basis. B items are those that fall between A and C items; they have moderate dollar volume.

3. In the not-too-distant past the decision on sourcing would have been based almost exclusively on price. Although price is still a significant factor in the decision, today, companies are more likely to place weight on the ability of the supplier to deliver reliable, high-quality goods. The nature of the relationship has also changed to allow for more cooperation between customer and supplier. Both the supplier and the customer realize that their mutual survival depends on jointly reducing costs and delivering greater value to the customer. To facilitate this type of communication and cooperation, firms are reducing the number of suppliers they purchase from and are attempting to purchase more standardized parts.

5. The cost of purchasing is not included because the purchase cost relates to the question "from whom to buy" rather than to the separate question "how many to buy." The latter question is the concern addressed by EOQ.

7. MRP overcomes the deficiency of ignoring relationships among inventory items by integrating interrelationships of units into the ordering process.

9. Significant benefits achieved by many firms using MPR include elimination of erratic production and back orders, streamlining scheduling and receiving operations, better utilization of labor, improved utilization of space, and reduction of inventory levels.

11.   Primary goals of JIT are:
      ■   elimination of any process which does not add value to
           the product
      ■   continuous improvement of production efficiency
      ■   reduction of total cost of production rather than merely
           the cost of purchasing

      JIT attempts to achieve these goals by working to:
      ■   eliminate the acquisition/production of inventories in
           excess of current needs
      ■   reduce lead/setup times
      ■   minimize product defects

13.   Manufacturing cells are u-shaped groupings of workers and
      machines. Benefits include reducing inventory storage,
      improving materials handling and flow, increasing machine
      utilization rates, maximizing worker communications, improving
      quality control, broadening worker skills, and increasing
      worker involvement in the work place.

15.   Major purposes of JIT are:
      a.   Increasing throughput, thereby minimizing the time from
           receiving customer orders to delivery of product. The
           theory is that less time results in lower costs.

      b.   Eliminating production and storage space not only
           minimizes unnecessary movements during production but
           also reduces tendency to allow inventory to sit idly in
           storage. The theory is that reducing unnecessary
           movements and storage time reduces production costs and
           inventory carrying costs.

      c.   Rearranging production facilities minimizes unnecessary
           movements and improves production flow. Aiming for zero
           defects reduces rework costs. The theory is that
           reducing time and movement and doing things right the
           first time minimizes energy and therefore cost.

17.   MRP and JIT systems are not compatible because MRP is a push
      system calling for production and storage of inventory not
      currently needed whereas JIT is a pull system which strives
      for complete elimination of inventory not currently needed.

19. Because variances represent "out of control" situations, in a JIT system the situation that creates a variance must be solved "on the spot." With JIT management of inventory, quality of processes and products must be very high because poor quality translates very quickly into missed shipments and backorders. Thus, in a JIT environment, problems that create (quantity) variances are solved immediately; at period end when variances would normally be examined, the cause and solution of the variance have already been addressed. For this reason, variance analysis contributes very little to control in a JIT-managed firm. Also, price variances are not likely to occur in such firms because major inputs are acquired from suppliers under long-term pricing agreements.

21. Backflush costing takes the production output based on a periodic inventory system and works backwards through the system with standard costs to assign production costs to inventory and cost of goods sold. Backflush costing is quicker and easier to apply than using a perpetual system and actual costing.

23. Research shows that about 90 percent of a product's life-cycle cost is determined during the development stage.

Exercises

25. Note: There are no "correct" answers to this question, particularly in regard to type B items. Below are possible answers.
    a. A, B
    b. A, B
    c. B, C
    d. A, B, C
    e. A, B
    f. C
    g. C
    h. C
    i. A, B
    j. C
    k. A, B

27. Carrying costs

Storage	$0.15
Handling	.05
Insurance	.06
Total	$0.26

29. a. EOQ, axles = $\sqrt{[(2 \times 2,000 \times \$20) \div \$.50]}$
       = <u>400</u>

    EOQ, wheels = $\sqrt{[(2 \times 4,000 \times \$36) \div \$3.00]}$
       = <u>310</u> (rounded)

b.   average inventory, axles = 400 ÷ 2 = <u>200</u>
      average inventory, wheels = 310 ÷ 2 = <u>155</u>

c.   The memo should address the fact that the EOQ model
      generates ordering quantities for axles and wheels that
      fail to reflect the relative quantities of the items
      needed for production. A rational inventory policy
      should have about twice as many wheels on hand as axles;
      this reflects the proportion demanded by production.

31. a.   Material quantity variance:
          Current standard
            Material A: (2,000 × 10 × $3.75) $ 75,000
            Material B: (2,000 × 10 × $4.90)   98,000
               Total $173,000
          Actual usage
            Material A: (21,000 × $3.75) $78,750
            Material B: (19,500 × $4.90)   95,550   174,300
                                                            $ 1,300 U

          ENC variance:
            Current standard $173,000
            Old standard
              Material A: (2,000 × 8 × $3.75) $ 60,000
              Material B: (2,000 × 12 × $4.90) 117,600   177,600
                                                            $ 4,600 F

b.   The effect of the engineering change was to reduce
      product cost by $4,600 in April from the level the
      company would have expected them to be without the ENC.
      The engineering change allowed the company to use more of
      the less expensive material and less of the more
      expensive material.

c.   The idea for the change could come from many sources:
      production personnel, marketing personnel, R&D projects
      personnel, or vendors. However, the actual change should
      be approved by the manager who is responsible for product
      design. Additionally, production and marketing personnel
      should be consulted in making the decision to make
      certain no important factors are overlooked (durability,
      appearance, perceived quality, or conversion cost).

33. a. & b.

Item	Unit cost	Volume sold		Cost × Volume	
Wet suit—Men's	$60.00	170		$10,200.00	
Wet suit—Women's	52.00	102	20%	5,304.00	
Meters & Connections	42.00	36	A	1,512.00	80%
Air tanks	36.00	42	Group	1,512.00	
Masks—Men's	4.00	280		1,120.00	
Flipper—Men's	3.00	320		960.00	
Underwater watches	25.00	32	30%	800.00	
Masks—Women's	3.40	172	B	584.80	12%
Flippers—Women's	2.50	210	Group	525.00	
Snorkels	1.20	420		504.00	
Wet suits—Children's	42.00	12		504.00	
Weights—Large	2.00	160		320.00	
Weights—Medium	1.50	180	50%	270.00	
Flippers—Children's	1.80	66	C	118.80	8%
Weight belts—Men's	1.80	63	Group	113.40	
Masks—Children's	2.80	40		112.00	
Weights—Small	1.25	64		80.00	
Weight belts—Women's	1.70	46		78.20	
Earplugs	.25	120		30.00	
Weight belts—Children's	1.20	12		14.40	
Totals		2,547		$24,662.60	

A $.20 \times 2,547 = 509.40$
B $.30 \times 2,547 = 764.10$
C $.50 \times 2,547 = 1,273.50$

c. Group A: Perpetual inventory system; daily counts and comparisons; and systematic monthly monitoring of EOQs, lead times and safety stocks.

Group B: Perpetual inventory system; monthly counts and comparisons; semi-annual monitoring of EOQs, lead times, and safety stocks.

Group C: Periodic inventory system; annual counts and gross profit analysis; a two-bin system for reordering.

35. a. $EOQ = \sqrt{[(2 \times 80,000 \times \$24) \div \$6]}$
         $= \underline{800}$ bags

b. Ordering costs: $(80,000 \div 800) \times \$24 = \$2,400$
    Carrying costs: $(800 \div 2) \times \$6 = \underline{2,400}$
    Total $\underline{\$4,800}$

c. Daily usage $= 80,000 \div 365 = 219.18$ bags
    $219.18 \times 30 = \underline{6,576}$ bags (rounded up)

    d.   Ordering costs: (80,000 ÷ 4,000) × $24 $ 480
         Carrying costs: (4,000 ÷ 2) × $6   12,000
            Total costs increase to $12,480

    e.   The company may get price discounts for this quantity, or
         this quantity may provide for more economical freight
         arrangements (i.e., railroad car). Alternatively, the
         vendor may only sell the cement in lots of 4,000 bags.

37. a.   D
    b.   U
    c.   D
    d.   T
    e.   T
    f.   T
    g.   D
    h.   T
    i.   T

39. a.   Material quantity variances:
         Current standard
             Rice 5 × 50,000 × $.02 $ 5,000.00
         Actual
             Rice 16,562 × 16 × $.02   5,299.84
                 Total $ 299.84 U

         Current standard
             Beans 7 × 50,000 × $.03 $10,500.00
         Actual
             Beans 21,250 × 16 × $.03   10,200.00
                 Variance $ 300.00 F

    b.   Rice (5 − 6) × 50,000 × $.02 $1,000 F
         Beans (7 − 6) × 50,000 × $.03 $1,500 U

    c.   The company may have made the change to respond to
         consumer preferences (more beans less rice translates
         into higher sales), because the firm wanted to change the
         nutrition content of the soup, or because of limited
         availability of rice in the required quantities and
         quality.

41.
  a. Raw & In-process Inventory (RIP)   24,904,000
     Material Purchase Price Variance   480
         Accounts Payable   24,904,480

     Accounts Payable   24,904,480
         Cash   24,904,480

b. Conversion Costs   2,918,000
    Accumulated Depreciation   321,000
    Cash   103,000
    Accounts Payable   2,494,000

  Accounts Payable   2,494,000
    Cash   2,494,000

c. Raw and In-Process
   Inventory (2,080,000 × $1.40)   2,912,000
   Conversion Cost Variance   6,000
    Conversion Costs   2,918,000

d. Conversion Costs   14,432,000
    Accumulated Depreciation   4,000,000
    Cash   9,325,000
    Accounts Payable   1,107,000

  Accounts Payable   1,107,000
    Cash   1,107,000

e. Raw and In-Process
   Inventory (10,320,000 × $1.40)   14,448,000
    Conversion Cost Variances   16,000
    Conversion Costs   14,432,000

Cases

43. a. The objectives for the general improvement of a production system as emphasized in the just-in-time (JIT) management philosophy include

- Flowing product continuously through the plant and minimizing the investment in raw materials, work-in-progress, and finished goods inventories
- Making production operations in the plant more efficient by redesigning work stations, simplifying the environment, and reducing both setup and lead times
- Increasing the attention to quality control, reducing obsolescence and waste and identifying non-value-added cost drivers (e.g., nonproductive labor) that can be eliminated

b.   Megafilters Inc. can take the following actions to ease
      the transition to a just-in-time (JIT) production system
      at the Illinois plant.

   ■   Communicate to employees, customers, and vendors the
        corporate objectives and plans for implementing the
        JIT production system

   ■   Elicit employee participation in implementing the
        JIT system and train employees on the necessary
        tools (e.g., computers)

   ■   Chart the production-process flows through the plant
        and develop statistical measurement and control
        procedures. Simplify processing and identify and
        alleviate cost drivers, non-value-added activities
        and waste

   ■   Obtain competitive bids and JIT proposals from
        several vendors for each material, selecting the few
        who will reduce lead times, increase the quality of
        the raw materials, and comply with strict delivery
        schedules

c.   Megafilters Inc. must establish the following appropriate
      relationships in order to successfully implement the
      just-in-time (JIT) production system.

   Vendors

   ■   Reduce the number of vendors to those who will be
        highly dependable and reliable

   ■   Commit the vendor to high quality standards by
        shifting responsibility for production problems to
        the suppliers (e.g., defective parts)

   Employees

   ■   Develop trust and communications with the employees
        to obtain a team participation in the initial plan
        and to elicit feedback in the future

   ■   Increase the employees' responsibility to assist in
        improving operations and quality while reducing cost
        drivers

   ■   Treat employees as partners in the process,
        eliciting their commitment

   Customers

   ■   Develop trust and communications for including the
        customers' participation in the initial plan and
        eliciting feedback

   ■   Ensure that Megafilters is fulfilling the customers'
        needs and demands

   ■   Build a team spirit through assurance that the
        company will meet the customers' demands at a
        competitive price. Employ the customer as a partner
        in the process (e.g., wait together for delayed
        deliveries, in order to keep costs at a minimum)

                                                        (CMA)

45.   a.   A JIT manufacturing system requires the establishment of manufacturing cells in the plant. The company has to adopt the philosophy of Total Quality Control (TQC). No scrap or waste is allowed. Inventory levels should be zero (because JIT is a demand pull approach). Workers in each cell are trained to perform various tasks within the cell. Therefore, idle time is not permissible. Finally, each cell is considered a decentralized center.

The Conventional System

Sales Price Per Unit for the Special Order $110
Relevant Manufacturing Costs Per Unit
          Direct Materials $40
          Direct Labor   30
          Variable Overhead   20   90
               Contribution Margin $ 20

Differential revenue of the special order is computed as follows: $110 × 100,000 units = $11,000,000
The differential costs to produce the special order are computed as follows: $90 × 100,000 units = $9,000,000
Therefore, the total contribution margin (profit) of the special order is $2,000,000 ($11,000,000 - $9,000,000)
Fixed manufacturing costs are irrelevant in this case.

The Just-in-Time System

Sales Price Per Unit of the Special Order $110
Relevant Manufacturing Costs Per Unit
          Direct Materials $40
          Variable Overhead   15   55
               Contribution Margin $ 55

The differential revenue of the special order is computed as follows: $110 × 100,000 units = $11,000,000
The differential costs to produce the special order are computed as follows: $55 × 100,000 units = $5,500,000
Therefore, the total contribution margin (profit) of the special order is $5,500,000 ($11,000,000 - $5,500,000).
Fixed manufacturing costs are irrelevant in this case.
Direct labor costs are considered fixed costs under JIT.

b.   The activity-based costing method allocates the cost pools of manufacturing overhead to various cost drivers and then to products based on the amount or number of other bases that each product consumes in various cost drivers.

The just-in-time philosophy has numerous objectives. Among these are the use of various cost drivers, zero inventory levels, total quality control, no idle time, no inefficiency, no non-value-added operations, continual improvements, and employee and worker involvement.

It is evident that a higher contribution margin results from the ABC method and the just-in-time philosophy. As illustrated in this case, the JIT method would result in a pricing decision that makes the company more competitive in the marketplace. The JIT approach will enable the company to sell its products at a lesser price while increasing the contribution margin.

[Copyright 1991 IMA (formerly NAA)]

Ethics and Quality Discussions

47. a.   The technologies mentioned in the problem affect the ordering and carrying costs of inventory. The changes mentioned should allow the firm to order in smaller economic lots. The technology would reduce purchasing transaction costs and improve communication with suppliers. This should facilitate more purchasing transactions at lower cost.

b.   The EOQ should decline. Although technology is likely to have little impact on carrying costs of most types of inventory (perishable items would be an exception), it is likely to impact ordering costs substantially. As ordering costs decline, the EOQ will also decline.

c.   Input from a variety of experts should be consulted. Following are some important sources of information:
vendors: on the feasibility of ordering in smaller quantities
transportation and freight experts: economy of transporting smaller order quantities
warehouse manager: on alternative uses of existing storage space
production manager: on any implications of lower inventory levels for production
material handling experts: on additional costs associated with more frequent deliveries and on the capacity of the facilities to handle more deliveries
information system experts: on technologies to economically manage increased information flow between the company and its suppliers

49. a. The examples clearly indicate the dependence of companies on their suppliers to control quality. For example, if a soda company purchases cans from an aluminum company, which contain shards of metal, quality of the final product is defective despite how well the company's internal processes may produce soda. Faulty inputs lead to defective output, and it doesn't matter whether the faults occur in the supplier's plant or the customer's plant.

     b. For many businesses it is the perception of quality that matters. It is also likely that the "actual" quality and the perceived quality sometimes diverge. Even though, in reality, no soda bottles may be contaminated with metal shards, if consumers think contamination exists sales will be adversely affected. Similarly, to the extent foreign objects in soda go undetected, actual poor quality may be perceived as high quality. However, in the long run, consumers' perceptions are not likely to deviate far from actual quality levels.

     c. There are ethical considerations in quality control of food products. The cases in which the consumer might not be able to detect the flaws create the ethical conflict.
       In those cases where quality failure would be obvious to the consumer, no ethical conflict exists because both ethics and economics mandate that such units be kept from consumers.
         However, with a slight imperfection in the product that could have negative health consequences, but not necessarily so, a company may perceive that it is economically better off not to scrap units in inventory or recall units that have been sold. The consequence of selling such units if no harm is caused the consumer is higher profits for the company. If consumers become ill the consequences are health-related problems and costs for consumers, and possible legal actions for the company.

51. a. Unions typify the historically hostile relations between managers and workers. Unions were founded on the basis of unfair treatment of workers by owners and managers. Consequently, the mistrust between management and unions is an artifact of that historical context--unions oppose managers and represent workers. Naturally, then, unions will be suspicious of any new initiatives by managers that require workers to cooperate with managers. Unions are simply not structured to accommodate or facilitate cooperation.

b. Ethics aside, managers have an obligation to not use quality as an excuse to fire workers or oppose unions. Doing so undermines their credibility and will render future attempts to instill real changes ineffective.

Ethically, managers have an obligation to not make workers the victims of their own quality and efficiency achievements. If workers use their own (private) knowledge as the basis for changes in the firms operations that improve quality and efficiency, managers must not exploit that knowledge; i.e., no manager can ask a worker to work himself out of a job.

c. Workers and managers are mutually dependent on the ability of their firms to compete in the global market place. Without cooperation between the two groups the company will not be able to adopt the strategies that are necessary to effectively compete. Workers have an obligation to utilize all of their skills and talents to improve the quality of their work and the output of the firm. This means workers are ethically obligated to make a good faith effort to cooperate with managers in devising and implementing new programs and to share their knowledge about the firm's products and processes.

CHAPTER 12
CONTROLLING NONINVENTORY COSTS

Questions

1. Cost control for any event is exerted before, during, and after that event. Control is exerted before the event to determine the expected cost and to provide a plan to achieve the expected cost. During an event, control is exerted so that the cost is incurred at the planned level. After an event, actual and planned performance are compared and explanations of differences are developed. By understanding why differences exist, managers can act to minimize future negative differences between the actual and planned amounts or to change processes so that positive differences can be maintained.

3. On-the-job training helps instill cost consciousness in employees by making employees aware of the significance of cost control. Training employees to perform their jobs correctly will tend to make employees recognize when processes could be performed better and often at less cost. Cost control suggestions should be encouraged and rewarded by employers. Also, training is an effective investment in human resources because workers can apply the concepts and skills they are learning directly to the jobs they are performing.

5. Companies can (a) pass along the costs as price increases to maintain the same income level; (b) decrease other costs to maintain the same income level; or (c) experience a decline in net income. Possibility (a) may not be an option if prices are highly fixed by competitive market forces, unless all firms in the industry respond in the same manner to the increased costs. Possibility (c) is generally unacceptable from any stakeholder point of view. Thus, the most rational way to cope with increased costs in an area over which little control can be effected is to try and better control costs in areas over which managers and employees have the most control.

7. A change in the quantity of supply does not necessarily cause the same impact as a change in the quantity of suppliers. If the number of suppliers increased, but the supply remained stable, prices would probably not fall. For instance, if weather causes crop damage, an increase in number of suppliers would not cause the price of lettuce or strawberries to decline.

9. This statement is probably true and, considering the headlines in newspapers and journals about cost control, it seems that managers in many organizations act in this manner. The real question is not whether cutting employees is the quickest way to reduce costs, but whether it is the most effective or efficient way to reduce costs. If an organization has expanded to the point at which many employees have redundant positions or are only giving part-time work for full-time pay, then cutting positions may be both effective and efficient. A decision to downsize, however, should be undertaken only after analyzing employee workloads and processes.

11. Activity-based management (ABM) should be an integral part of cost control because it provides a consumer's perspective on cost control issues. At the heart of ABM is the idea that activities should be examined based on their effects on customer value. Thus, ABM contributes to cost control by identifying which activities should be considered for reduction or elimination by minimizing or eliminating activities that created little or no customer value.

13. By cooperating with members of the supply chain, an organization creates an opportunity for interorganizational cost management. Sharing information allows suppliers to offer alternatives that would lower the organization's costs and result in reduced prices to customers. Additionally, outsourcing opportunities may be identified for circumstances in which a supplier can provide a service, commodity, or part, at a lower cost than the organization can produce it itself.

15. Careful capital budgeting analysis is made before committing the firm to long-run costs such as investing in plant assets. Control of committed costs is also accomplished through comparing actual with expected results during the post-investment audit. Committed costs may also be controlled by seeking ways to enhance the productivity of the human or physical capital.

17. Extensive investment in automated technology affects a firm's cost structure by increasing committed fixed costs. Thus, a negative consequence is that, as the proportion of committed fixed costs to total costs rises, fewer and fewer costs are avoidable as sales fall. The result can be substantial operating losses in economic downturns. Such losses can threaten the ability of the firm to remain solvent and survive. Even so, as an industry becomes more and more competitive, firms will make increased investment in automated technology to control operating costs and quality. The challenge for such an industry then becomes finding ways to maintain sales volume during economic slumps.

19. When setting discretionary cost appropriations, managers should consider:
    - Which discretionary activities should be funded to help management effectively and efficiently achieve its objectives.
    - Whether the benefits of the discretionary activities exceed the cost appropriations.
    - Whether projected profits are adequate to support the planned discretionary activities.

21. For some discretionary costs, this result may be praiseworthy if the funded activities are producing satisfactory outcomes, which are often difficult to measure. However, a manager should not be praised if cost savings relate to discretionary activities that are critical, such as preventive maintenance, safety programs, and pollution abatement programs.

23. Efficiency is a measure of the degree to which the actual yield ratio (actual output ÷ actual input) conforms to the desired yield ratio (planned output ÷ planned input). Effectiveness is a measure of the degree to which a goal or objective is achieved.

25. To measure the efficiency of a discretionary cost requires both an input and an output measure. Efficiency further requires a predictable cause and effect relationship between input and output. Input costs are readily measured, however, outputs may not be readily available. When they are available or when surrogates can be identified, there still may be a lack of confidence about the cause and effect relationship between input and output for most discretionary costs.

    To measure the effectiveness of a discretionary activity, a monetary or nonmonetary output measure must be available or devised. Sometimes a surrogate measure of an activity's output can be agreed upon. Effectiveness can then be measured by comparing actual output to planned output (i.e., actual output ÷ planned output).

27. A planning budget is fixed at a given level of output volume. Often, the actual output level does not equal the planned level and, therefore, costs will differ from those budgeted because of volume differences. If managers have no control over volume, a flexible budget should be prepared for costs at the actual activity level and is used to evaluate managerial performance.

29. Program budgeting relates resource inputs to service outputs.
     Rather than a traditional approach that initially focuses on
     the quantity of input activities and resources needed, program
     budgeting begins by translating objectives into desired output
     results, providing a basis for measuring effectiveness from
     the outset. Program budgeting also analyzes sets of
     alternative activities and their projected costs to determine
     which set and related costs will best meet organizational
     objectives.

Exercises

31. a. 4   f. 3
     b. 6   g. 10
     c. 1   h. 8
     d. 5   i. 9
     e. 2   j. 7

33. a. Cost understanding
     b. Cost containment
     c. Cost avoidance or cost containment
     d. Cost reduction or cost avoidance
     e. Cost avoidance (long-term; discuss, however, the
         significant costs incurred to effect this move)
     f. Cost understanding
     g. Cost reduction or cost avoidance

35. a. D; is the definition of a discretionary cost
     b. C; relates to the basic infrastructure of the
         organization and is best controlled prior to incurrence
     c. C; relates to organizational capacity to make products or
         perform services
     d. C; are unavoidable and related to fundamental plant
         assets
     e. D; is often difficult to describe the nature of the
         input/output relationship for these costs
     f. D; are generally costs that can be reduced in the short
         run without adversely impacting the long-run viability of
         the organization
     g. C; is the definition of a committed cost
     h. D; is often difficult to specify exactly what outcome is
         expected from incurring the cost or how much cost is
         optimal
     i. D; are incurred for support or peripheral activities
     j. D; is difficult to know what the optimal funding level is
         because it is difficult or impossible to specify what the
         outcomes are or what the yield is for cost incurrence

37. a. Revenue generated from yellow page advertising; number of calls received mentioning yellow page advertising

b. Labor cost savings; reduction in collection cycle; reduction in unbilled expenses; decrease in customer complaints about charges on bills

c. Extent to which strategic planning has been implemented in the firm; dollars of cost savings generated by strategic planning

d. Increase in employee and client satisfaction; improvement in flow of people; increase in number of people using the lobby area

e. Increase in customer satisfaction; decrease in customer complaints; increase in maternity care

f. Number of patient hours of treatment on the machine; number of new patients acquired because the hospital now has the machine

g. Increase in employee satisfaction; increase in employee retention rate; decrease in absenteeism rate

39. a.
Goal	300 new students
Actual achievement	325 new students
Goal exceeded by	25 new students

The department was very effective in meeting its goal.

b. Yield goal: ($400,000 ÷ 300) = 1 student for each $1,333 expended.

Actual efficiency ($460,000 ÷ 325) = 1 student for each $1,415 expended. The department was operationally inefficient in pursuing its objectives.

c. The department should also be evaluated on the quality of admits. At date of admission, quality could be measured using standardized test scores (such as the SAT or ACT) and high school grade point averages. After admission, quality can be measured by GPA and job placement or entrance into graduate school. Additionally, the department should be evaluated on student satisfaction with the college by reviewing retention rates. The department should also be evaluated on efforts to achieve demographic diversity. By using a variety of measures, the effectiveness and efficiency of the department can be viewed on both a short-term and long-term basis.

41. a.   For the Typing Department:
           Planned efficiency = $114,000 ÷ 40,000 pages =
           $2.85 per page
           Actual efficiency = $109,760 ÷ 29,400 pages = $3.73
           per page
       For the external agency:
           Actual efficiency = $2,875 ÷ 2,500 = $1.15 per page

     b.   Effectiveness = 29,400 pages typed ÷ 40,000 pages
           expected = 73.5%

     c.   One possible explanation is that the external agency
           personnel were not disturbed during business hours with
           tasks in addition to typing the outsourced letters. The
           in-house employees at Lucinda's may have additional
           responsibilities such as answering the phone, copying
           documents, responding to specific client requests, and so
           forth. The external agency may even be a virtual
           organization, in that it uses individuals who do not come
           into an office (with its related distractions) and simply
           perform their assignments at home and forward them to the
           external agency. Thus, these individuals may be
           considered subcontractors and so the agency does not need
           to pay fringe benefits, have a posh office setting, or
           possibly even have the committed costs of a vast array of
           equipment.

     d.   The pros of outsourcing all typing for a large
           organization are that the individuals are generally very
           experienced and punctual; fringe benefits do not have to
           be paid; and plant assets (such as computers and work
           stations) do not have be provided. Alternatively, if
           there are questions about what is being typed or how it
           should be typed, there may be difficulty in communicating
           between the typing firm and the organization's personnel
           who have requested the typing. Turnaround may also be
           impossible if something is needed immediately.

43. a.   **Departmental Budget** (1,050 hours)
           Management salaries $19,500.00
           Worker wages (1,050 × $15)   15,750.00
           Utilities [$3,700 + (1,050 × $.45)]   4,172.50
           Maintenance [$1,000 + (1,050 × $.70)]   1,735.00
           Supplies [$7,500 + (1,050 × $9.40)]   17,370.00
           Equipment depreciation   6,750.00
           Total budget $65,277.50

b.   No, the figures would be incorrect for comparison purposes. The budget would need to be adjusted to reflect the actual hours of 1,120.

Revised Departmental Budget (1,120 hours)

Management salaries	$19,500.00
Worker wages (1,120 × $15)	16,800.00
Utilities [$3,700 + (1,120 × $.45)]	4,204.00
Maintenance [$1,000 + (1,120 × $.70)]	1,784.00
Supplies [$7,500 + (1,120 × $9.40)]	18,028.00
Equipment depreciation	6,750.00
Total budget	$67,066.00

45. a.   An architectural firm would spend more on prevention and appraisal than the typical firm. The consequences for external failure can be severe: a faulty building plan could translate to loss of life and massive property damage. To avoid such consequences, firms are likely to invest heavily in training and review.

b.   Services provided by a hair salon have substantially lower external risks compared with some industries, such as health care or architecture. Also the technology is very low-tech compared to that of other industries. In general, the consequences of external failure are relatively insignificant (in the scheme of things, but possibly not to the individual). Thus, this type of firm would likely spend relatively less on prevention and appraisal than the other types of firms addressed in this problem.

c.   A heavy equipment manufacturer would invest heavily in product and process design because product quality is generally determined by expenditures made prior to production. Consequently, this type of firm will spend heavily on prevention and appraisal, but will expect to have some internal and external failures.

d.   In a health maintenance organization, an internal or external failure can mean loss of life, permanent injury, or unnecessary suffering. Further, through malpractice damages, failure costs can be extraordinarily high. For these reasons, HMOs would spend relatively high amounts for prevention and appraisal and *expect* relatively low expenditures for internal and external failure.

Chapter 12
Controlling Noninventory Costs

Problems

47. a. CU
     b. CU
     c. CA
     d. CU
     e. CU
     f. CA or CR
     g. CA
     h. CR
     i. CU
     j. CA
     k. CC
     l. CA

49. a. Cost understanding and cost avoidance are demonstrated in
         the response. Ms. Frankel does an excellent job of
         relating the activities required to fill the order for
         the California State University system to costs incurred
         in her publishing company.

     b. The regulations that must be complied with are
         voluminous. Because the purchaser is a unit of the State
         of California, it must comply with a significant number
         of procedural policies that exist for all state bodies.
         The purchasing department also has some federal
         regulations and some in-house policies with which it must
         comply.

     c. Bureaucracies work best for high volume transactions.
         Centralization of authority and control through detailed
         policies works well to standardize procedures and
         standardize services. The policies are surrogates for
         individual authority and judgment. This arrangement does
         not work well in low volume, unique transactions, and the
         arrangement is not flexible or sensitive to the
         circumstances of individual transactions. In fact, the
         arrangement looks ridiculous in this example. The
         transaction costs for purchasing this book must far
         exceed the price of the book. This is indicative of
         opportunity to cut costs. By removing many of the
         regulations and policies for small transactions, the
         State of California could save millions of tax dollars.

51. a.   This change is intended to increase efficiency; the patient will receive the same procedure as before, but with a shorter hospital stay. This is an example of cost avoidance or cost reduction. Costs that otherwise would have been incurred for a longer hospital stay are avoided.

     b.   This change increases both effectiveness and efficiency; the success rate of the operation is increased and subsequent treatment for infection is avoided. This example reflects cost reduction: decreasing the infection rate reduced the cost of the average treatment.

     c.   This change increases the efficiency of the operation. Fewer days in the hospital are required. This change represents cost reduction because the costs associated with a longer hospital stay are avoided.

     d.   This change results in an increase in efficiency. Fewer days in the hospital are required by completing the blood work earlier. This change represents cost understanding and cost reduction. Although a cost increase may have been incurred to get blood tests returned more quickly, this increase would be overwhelmed by the shorter hospital stay.

     e.   This change may have impacted both effectiveness and efficiency. The anti-nausea drug may have increased both the rate of success of the chemotherapy and decreased the average length of the hospital stay--increasing efficiency. This change represents both cost understanding and cost avoidance/reduction. By incurring higher costs for drugs, the length of the hospital stay and its associated costs are reduced.

53. a. $7,800 \times .985 = \underline{7,683}$ flawless gaskets per kwh

     b.   Achieved efficiency per kwh = $(1,390,000 - 14,000) \div 175$ = $\underline{7,863}$ gaskets per kwh which exceeds the standard by 180 flawless gaskets per kwh.

     Achieved effectiveness is equal to 1% flaws ($14,000 \div 1,390,000$) versus the expected 1.5% rate of flaws. Thus, the machine is more effective in producing flawless output than claimed.

c.   kwh at standard efficiency: [(1,390,000 - 14,000) ÷
      7,800] = 176.4 kwh.

      Standard kwh   176.40
      Actual kwh   175.00
      Kwh saved   1.40
      Cost per kwh   x $1.60
      Cost savings $ 2.24

d.   An automobile manufacturer would want zero defects in the
      gaskets it purchases and would expect the vendor to have
      sufficient quality control measures to virtually assure
      this.

55. a.   A flexible budget allows management to directly compare
           the actual cost of operations with budgeted costs for the
           activity achieved. It assists management in evaluating
           the effects of varying levels of activity on costs,
           profits, and cash position, thus aiding in the choice of
           the level of operation for planning purposes.
                The flexible budgets presented are based on three
           different activity measures, none of which coincide with
           the actual level of performance for November. The budget
           must be restated to a level of activity that matches the
           actual results. The fixed and variable components of the
           mixed costs must be segregated and a budgeted cost
           calculated for the level of activity attained.

     b.   Sales salaries are the only cost that varies perfectly
           with number of salespersons ($90,000 ÷ 100 = $900).
           Following are costs items and their variable cost per
           sales order:
           Sales commissions $300
           Sales travel   100 ($50,000 assumed fixed)
           Sales office expense   30 ($400,000 assumed fixed)
           Shipping expense   100 ($500,000 assumed fixed)
           Total variable cost $530 per sales order

c.

Muir Wood Products
Selling Expense Report-November

Monthly Expenses	Budget	Actual	Variance	
Adver. & promo.	$1,500,000	$1,450,000	$50,000	F
Admin. salaries	75,000	80,000	5,000	U
Sales salaries[1]	81,000	92,000	11,000	U
Sales commissions[2]	447,000	460,000	13,000	U
Salesperson travel[3]	194,000	185,000	9,000	F
Sales off. expense[4]	448,000	500,000	52,000	U
Shipping expense[5]	660,000	640,000	20,000	F
Total	$3,405,000	$3,407,000	$ 2,000	U

[1]($90,000 ÷ 100) × 90 = $81,000

[2]($450,000 ÷ $15,000,000) × $14,900,000 = $218,800

[3]Change in cost: $225,000 - $200,000 = $25,000
  Change in sales $s: $17,500,000 - $15,000,000 = $2,500,000
  Variable cost per dollar of sales = change in cost ÷ change in activity level = $25,000 ÷ $2,500,000 = $.01 per sales $
  Fixed cost at 75-person level: $200,000 - ($15,000,000 × .01) = $50,000
  Fixed cost at 90-person level: ($50,000 ÷ 100) × 90 = $45,000
  Total travel budget: $45,000 fixed + (14,900,000 × .01) = $45,000 + $149,000 = $194,000

[4]Change in cost: $452,500 - $445,000 = $7,500
  Change in number of orders: 1,750 - 1,500 = 250
  Variable cost per order: $7,500 ÷ 250 = $30
  Fixed cost: $445,000 - (1,500 × $30) = $400,000
  Total office expense budget: $400,000 + (1,600 × $30) = $448,000

[5]Change in cost: $675,000 - $650,000 = $25,000
  Change in number of units: 17,500 - 15,000 = 2,500
  Variable cost per unit: $25,000 ÷ 2,500 = $10.00
  Fixed cost: $650,000 - (15,000 × $10) = $500,000
  Total shipping expense budget: $500,000 + (16,000 × $10) = $660,000

d.   Sales salaries ÷ number of salespersons = $92,000 ÷ 90 =
          $1,022 fixed cost (rounded)
      [**Note:** to estimate the actual variable cost portion of
      the mixed costs, the fixed portion of the mixed cost was
      assumed to equal the budgeted amount]
      Actual variable cost per sales order: Commissions ÷
          Number of orders = $460,000 ÷ 1,600 = $287.50
      Variable travel ÷ Number of orders = ($185,000 -
          $50,000) ÷ 1,600 = $84.38 (rounded)
      Variable office expense ÷ Number of orders = ($500,000 -
          $400,000) ÷ 1,600 = $62.50
      Variable shipping expense ÷ Number of orders = ($640,000
          - $500,000) ÷ 1,600 = $87.50

e.   To comment on effectiveness would require knowledge of a
      target sales figure. If such a target had been less than
      or equal to $14,900,000, the salespersons could have been
      considered effective. Otherwise, a degree of
      effectiveness of less than 100% must be assigned.
          The manager of sales expenses must be considered to
      be slightly less than 100% efficient as evidenced by the
      $2,000 unfavorable variance presented in Part c.
                                              (CMA adapted)

Cases

57. a.   Some considerations for the bookstore include the
          following:

   - Exercise prudent cost management over discretionary
     costs. One of the more significant discretionary costs
     is advertising.

   - Maximize use of technology. Although book handling is
     inherently a labor intensive exercise, transaction
     processing related to sales, purchases, and repurchases
     can be highly automated to save labor costs.

   - Institute programs to reduce employee turnover. Because
     many employees may be students, employee turnover can
     be very high. Employee turnover increases specific
     costs such as employee training, quality failure costs,
     and unemployment taxes.

   - Arrange floor space to minimize book handling costs and
     to facilitate the flow of students.

   - Work closely with professors to ascertain which books
     will be used in the upcoming semester and which will
     not be used again.

   - Develop associations with book wholesalers to market
     books that are no longer adopted by the local
     university.

   - Encourage professors to adopt the same book for
     multiple sections of the same class to realize
     economies of scale in purchasing and shipping.

   - Provide incentives to students to purchase books early
     so that the workload can be spread across more time and
     be handled by fewer employees.

   - Use temporary rather than permanent employees to handle
     busy season work.

   - Find innovative ways to manage freight costs. Examine
     alternative modes of transportation. By ordering
     earlier, slower and less expensive freight delivery
     modes can be used.

   - Rent temporary warehouse space to handle the bulge in
     inventory that accompanies the start and end of school
     terms.

b. Some considerations for book publishers include:
- Maximize the life cycle length of each publication so that fixed costs can be spread across more units.
- Manage the product mix so that unprofitable publications are eliminated.
- Manage the number of publications that are overseen by each editor.
- Adopt labor-saving technology to improve quality and reduce labor costs in the publishing operation.
- Make professors aware that there are costs to providing teaching supplements and that such costs must eventually be passed on to students.
- Conduct market research to determine what students and professors desire in terms of textbook features, content, and supplements. This will minimize expenditures on unprofitable and low volume products.
- Minimize the number of drafts of each book that must be printed prior to printing the final version.
- Focus quality control on each textbook while it is in draft form to eliminate changes that are very costly to make in later stages of production.
- Consider the use of part-time editors and other employees.
- Consider outsourcing those aspects of operations that can be accomplished more efficiently and effectively by outside vendors.
- Manage the purchasing of paper and other inputs to minimize handling costs and maximize purchase discounts.
- Concentrate on developing JIT production capability to minimize production of books that are currently not in demand. This will reduce storage needs and costs associated with carrying inventory.
- Adopt the latest technologies in cost management (e.g., activity-based costing).

c.   Students can
  - Share textbooks with a friend or acquaintance who is taking the same class. This approach can effectively cut the cost of purchasing books in half.
  - Avoid purchasing supplements and other materials that are not required by the instructor.
  - Purchase their required textbooks from students rather than the bookstore. This eliminates the bookstore markup.
  - Purchase the paperback editions rather than hardback textbooks.
  - Sell textbooks to the bookstore or other wholesalers at the end of the semester.
  - Use electronic versions of the textbook rather than paper versions to eliminate publication costs.
  - Exert pressure on professors to eliminate the use of unnecessary supplements.

d.   College textbooks are different today for three major reasons. First, the subject matter of many disciplines has changed dramatically in the past 20 years. Second, the technology available to publishers has advanced and allows more sophisticated products to be developed. Third, the market has become extraordinarily competitive and has forced textbook publishers to offer more comprehensive products to attract and maintain market share.

59.   To: Mary Ross
       From: Barry Stein
       Re: Explanation of November 2000 Variances

a.   The revenue mix variance resulted from a higher proportion of participants being eligible for discounts. The budgeted revenue was based on 30 percent of the participants taking the discount; but, during November, 45 percent of those attending the courses received discounts. As a result, the weighted average fee dropped from $145.50 to $143.25.

b.   The most significant implication of the revenue mix variance is that the proportion of discount fees has increased by 50 percent. If the increase represents a trend, the implications for future profits could be serious as revenues per participant day will decline while costs are likely to remain steady or increase.

c.   The revenue timing difference was caused by early registrations for the December program to be held in Cincinnati. The early registrations resulted from the combined promotional mailing for both the Chicago and Cincinnati programs. These early registrations have been prematurely recognized as revenue during November.

d.   The November revenue recognition of early registrations
     for December courses is inappropriate, and, thus,
     revenues during December may be lower than expected.

e.   The primary cause of the unfavorable total expense
     variance were additional food charges, course materials,
     and instructor fees. Although these quantity variances
     are unfavorable, the increased costs of $10,400 are more
     than offset by the additional revenues of $40,740 with
     which these items are associated.

f.   The favorable food price variance was determined by
     multiplying the difference between the budgeted and
     actual price per participant day times the actual
     participant days. The actual price per participant day
     was determined by dividing the actual food charges by the
     total participant days ($32,000 ÷ 1,280).

g.   Although the promotional piece had a $5,000 unfavorable
     impact on November expenses, further promotion of the
     Cincinnati program will not be needed. Thus, the $20,000
     budgeted for this purpose in December will not be spent,
     thus lowering that month's expenses.
         The promotion timing difference represents an
     incorrect matching of costs and revenue. The costs
     allocated to the Cincinnati program should be reflected
     on the December statement of operations to be matched
     against the December program.

h.   The course development variance is unfavorable to the
     November budget, but its overall impact on the company
     cannot be determined until such time as the level of
     acceptance of the new course is experienced.

                                                      (CMA)

Ethics and Quality Discussions

61. This problem presents a conflict between the quantity of service and the quality of service provided. The empowerment of counselors will allow counselors to make decisions regarding the families they serve without the added time involved in obtaining administrative approval. Similarly, establishing a set time limit for meeting with families and abolishing review processes will also save time. However, these safeguards were established originally to ensure that only high quality services were provided to the agency's clients.

    On balance, the changes outlined will allow the agency to be more efficient (more clients served per counselor), but less effective (less resolution of client problems). It is extremely difficult to determine whether it is more ethical to be effective or efficient in providing social services. There are ethical merits to both performance dimensions. To the extent that only qualified, experienced people are employed by the agency, the changes instituted are ethically sound. Alternatively, if the employees are inexperienced, or marginally qualified, the drop in quality of services may be so profound as to be ethically objectionable.

63. Each student will have a different answer to this question. No solution provided.

65. Each student will have a different answer to this question. No solution provided.

67. a. Each student will have different answers to these questions. Some possible explanations for being over budget, however, include special effects, high actor salary demands, delays in shooting, and script rewriting.

Chapter 12
Controlling Noninventory Costs

CHAPTER 13
CONTROLLING COSTS IN THE CHANGING WORKPLACE

Questions

1. Proponents of open-book management argue that the open-book approach helps employees understand how their work activities affect the costs and revenues of the firm. With this understanding, employees can adopt or change work practices to either increase revenues or decrease costs.

3. Games make learning financial information fun and relevant. Also, games provide a way for financial information to be provided to workers in a simplified format. Workers learn that use of financial information allows them to play the game better.

5. Accounting personnel must be prepared to provide simplified accounting information that is relevant to the game. A simplified information system will be easier to grasp for unsophisticated employees. Also, accounting personnel must be prepared to provide training to workers so that they will understand the information they are given. Furthermore, the accountants must develop the mindset that they are conveyors, rather than guardians, of information. Finally, accountants must participate in the development of performance measures that are appropriate for the games that are developed.

7. There are three major trends driving the increased use of BPR: the rapid pace of advancements in technology; the need to increase quality of operations to satisfy consumer demands; and the increased focus on price competition brought about by global competition.

9. The theory of constraints is a management philosophy about focusing managerial attention on bottlenecks (or constraints) to improve performance. The foundation beliefs are that
   1. every system has constraints that limit output;
   2. management of the constraints determines the performance of the system;
   3. any system has only one to a few constraints at any particular time; and
   4. the assumed objective of managing constraints is to maximize throughput.

11. Performance measures are used to evaluate the effectiveness of
     managing constrained resources. Evaluations based on these
     performance measures give managers an incentive to effectively
     manage constrained resources.

13. Today, competition is as much between value chains as it is
     between individual firms. Interorganizational management of
     costs and cooperation is required for one value chain to
     effectively compete with other value chains.

15. Outsourcing creates greater reliance on other firms. This
     increased reliance reflects a decrease in control management
     has over the ultimate product or service that is produced. If
     the wrong vendor is selected, quality problems can develop,
     and shortages of the outsourced item can occur because of late
     deliveries. Also, by outsourcing, a firm may lose the ability
     to perform a particular function that may prove later to be
     crucial to its survival.
         In general, firms should never outsource functions that
     represent core competencies. These functions are too critical
     to the firm's long-term survival; reliance on suppliers to
     perform these functions would be too risky.

17. Target costing and value engineering facilitate discussion on
     cost management between supplier and customer firms. Often
     the target costing system of one firm is used to develop
     target costs for specific components. These target costs are
     then used as a basis for negotiation or even collaboration
     with suppliers to reduce costs. Used in this manner, the
     target costing system is used to pressure suppliers to
     participate in cost management.

19. Downsizing is the common term used for management actions that
     reduce employment and restructure operations as a response to
     competitive pressures. For example, business process
     reengineering leads to greater efficiency of operations and a
     need for fewer personnel. Adoption of advanced technology to
     improve quality also reduces headcount. Training workers to
     be more efficient further reduces the demand for employees.
     As indicated in the Laborforce 2000 survey, downsizing is
     related to management initiatives to improve profitability and
     quality, increase competitiveness, and reduce costs.

21. The globalization of markets has created a more diverse workforce. With operations distributed around the world, many firms now have employees who speak divergent languages, have different cultures and values, and have different religious beliefs and work habits. By simply employing local people in widely distributed operations, firms have greatly diversified their workforces.

The accounting system must play a larger role in firms with diverse employees. Because the interpretation of accounting information is not contingent on local language or local culture, accounting can serve as an important communication medium for diverse employees. Thus, accounting is an ideal international technical language. Because communication in other languages is more difficult, an increased reliance on communication in the accounting language is likely.

23. The use of cross-functional teams creates two new demands on the accounting function. The first is a requirement for accountants to participate in cross-functional teams and provide a financial perspective on decisions. The second requirement is that the accounting function develops means to evaluate the performance of teams as well as the performance of individuals.

Exercises

25. Currently employees in the production department are not evaluated or compensated based on the quality of their work. Open-book management can be used to change the behaviors of employees by changing their incentives.

The first step in implementing open-book management in the production department would be to develop performance measures of quality. Traditional measures such as scrap, waste, rework costs, and nontraditional measures—such as level of customer satisfaction with quality—could be developed. Although dollars could be used as the unit of measurement, physical units would be more readily grasped by the workers (for example, pounds of materials wasted rather than dollars of materials wasted).

The second step in the implementation of open-book management would be to train workers to understand how the performance measures capture their actions and how they can affect the measures. The training sessions should precede the actual use of the new performance measures.

The final step in the implementation would be to link the pay of the workers to the new performance measures. In this step, the workers are provided with incentives to improve quality performance measurements. Training sessions would be required to help workers understand how they can improve their performance rewards by improving the quality of their output.

Finally, a game could be devised to use in training sessions that would demonstrate to the workers how quality measurement and employee rewards are linked and how changes in the performance measures lead to changes in the payoffs.

27. a.   Out-of-pocket costs
          DM $140,000
          DL   150,000
          Variable OH   72,000
          Fixed OH   50,000
                                          $412,000

     b.   Opportunity costs: $6,000 CM from producing gravel
          grinders

     c.   Cost to make: $412,000 + $6,000 = $418,000
          Cost to outsource: 100 × $4,200 = 420,000
          Advantage to insourcing $ 2,000

29. a.   A car dealer's contribution to an automobile value chain
          is more modest than that of the manufacturer.
          Furthermore, the car dealer is probably unable to exert
          much influence on the manufacturer to change its
          operations in any material manner. Thus the car dealer
          is not in an optimal position to influence other
          important firms in its value chain.

     b.   Like the car dealer, the small manufacturing company is
          not in a favorable position to influence other firms in
          its value chain. However, the firm can evaluate
          alternative suppliers of materials and can consider
          alternative marketing channels to get its product to
          consumers.

     c.   The large paper manufacturer may benefit substantially
          from value chain analysis. By virtue of its size, it can
          likely exert substantial influence over both its
          suppliers and its distribution channels. Therefore, this
          firm could benefit greatly from value chain cost
          analysis.

     d.   This firm must be effective in value-chain analysis, and
          because it competes on the basis of price, it must obtain
          its required components at the lowest cost possible.
          Because the firm buys components in large volumes, it is
          in a position to influence its suppliers and distribution
          channels. Thus, value-chain cost analysis could be very
          beneficial for this firm.

31. a.   An electrical engineer would be useful in determining
          whether the power infrastructure of potential site
          locations is adequate and what costs might be incurred to
          obtain the power necessary to operate the factory.

     b.   A labor expert could help determine whether alternative
          site locations offered the necessary labor skills and
          help estimate the potential labor cost savings from
          relocating the plant from California.

c. A mechanical engineer could help determine how operations
    would be arranged in the new plant, how existing
    equipment could be integrated with new equipment in the
    Mexican facility, and the production technology that
    would be appropriate for the new facility.

d. The accountant could help management estimate costs
    associated with various aspects of the relocation
    decision. For example, the accountant could estimate the
    following: costs of closing the existing factory,
    expenses necessary to help existing employees find
    alternative employment, costs of moving machinery and
    equipment to the new plant location, and cost savings
    to be generated by moving operations to Mexico.

e. A production manager could provide general information
    about the desirability of alternative site locations in
    terms of obtaining necessary inputs and shipping
    completed components. The production manager would also
    help determine what equipment must be purchased and the
    size and characteristics of the new facility that would
    be built in Mexico as well as the general layout of the
    new facility.

f. A corporate finance specialist could help estimate how
    much capital would be necessary to fund the new plant and
    how much capital could be released from sale of the
    existing plant. This person could also help determine
    how to finance the move and the acquisition of the new
    facility.

Problems

33. a.   Costs of insourcing:

Salaries & wages (avoidable)	$1,950,000
Office supplies	350,000
Occupancy costs	300,000
Selling and Administration	450,000
Depreciation	90,000
Total	$3,140,000

Costs of outsourcing:

Price from trucking firm	$2,500,000
Salaries and wages	150,000
Materials	100,000
Occupancy costs	300,000
Office supplies	50,000
Selling and Administration	56,000[*]
Depreciation	90,000
Total	$3,246,000

Advantage of insourcing: $3,246,000 - $3,140,000
$$= \underline{\$106,000}$$

[*] -$50,000 + ($12,000 × 3) + ($15,000 × 2)
         + ($10,000 × 4)

Note that a more efficient solution is based on only
the relevant costs (the costs that differ between
the alternatives):

Advantage of insourcing computed using relevant costs:

Price of outsourcing contract saved	$2,500,000
Labor cost savings sacrificed	(1,800,000)
Office supplies savings lost	(300,000)
Materials cost saved	100,000
Selling and administration savings lost	(394,000)
Advantage of insourcing	$ 106,000

b.   Some of the concerns other managers might have include

■   how the cost shifted from the Distribution
         Department will affect the evaluations of their
         departments,

■   how the transfer of personnel will affect their
         operations,

■   what the behavioral implications might be of
         shifting personnel and their responsibilities,

■   how reliable the freight company is relative to
         the Distribution department, and

■   whether the new arrangement creates any new
         managerial responsibilities.

Cases

35.   a.
Mallory's gross profit has declined from $160 to only $45 within the past year. At the same time, the industry average gross profit declined at a much slower rate: from $140 to $75. The decline in the average gross profit of the industry signals that the industry has become more price competitive and the larger decline for Mallory indicates that Mallory was unable to achieve cost reductions at the same pace as the industry achieved cost reductions.

For the first quarter of 1999, Mallory had a market share of approximately 13 percent (4,200 ÷ 32,000). Even though total industry unit sales were higher in the first quarter of 2000 than in the first quarter of 1999, Mallory's unit sales slipped and Mallory's market share dropped to about 8.6 percent (3,450 ÷ 40,000). This information indicates Mallory's selling price did not drop as fast as the industry average and sales were lost as a result. This is confirmed by calculating average sales price for Mallory for the first quarter of 1999, $1,525 ($6,405,000 ÷ 4,200), and comparing that price to the price for the first quarter of 2000, $1,350 ($4,657,500 ÷ 3,450). Thus, Mallory's sales price dropped from $1,525 to $1,350 while the industry average price dropped from $1,640 to $1,310. Although Mallory's price was well below the industry average in the first quarter of 1999, it was well above that average for the first quarter of 2000. This was the main reason unit sales and market share declined over the past year.

Because Mallory has no quality or functionality advantage over other industry competitors, the company must find ways to reduce its price to regain market share and unit sales. To reduce its price, the company must find ways to substantially reduce its costs.

b.

Several ways to reduce costs are evident. First, Mallory produces about 83 percent of its components. This is much higher than the industry average of 57 percent. Thus, Mallory should consider outsourcing some components. Second, Mallory should consider relocating the most labor-intensive operations to sites that have lower labor costs. The two major competitors that moved to China obviously did so to obtain a labor cost advantage. Mallory must find some way to match its competitors in reducing labor costs. Another possibility is for Mallory to consider acquiring more machine-intensive production technology to reduce the labor content of its transmissions. A third cost-reduction approach is to consider the application of business process reengineering to redesign production operations for greater efficiency. A fourth possibility is to redesign the transmission to remove costs. A target costing system could be applied to develop target costs for each major component. The   target costs of components could be used as a basis for negotiating prices with vendors for outsourced components. Mallory has less opportunity than other firms to use value chain analysis to remove costs because the company presently produces a very high percentage of all transmission components.

Finally, the company might consider developing incentives for internal cost reduction. Open-book management techniques could be applied to create incentives and generate downward pressure on costs.

Ethics and Quality Discussion

37. a.   The success of price-based competition is linked to the cost structure of the competitor. If GM has higher costs than its rivals, it will not be able to successfully use price-based competition. Its rivals will be able to underprice products with similar quality and functionality and take market share from GM.

b.   It is difficult to imagine that greater flexibility to outsource could have anything but a positive impact on quality. Because GM would always have the choice to make components that can't be obtained from a vendor with the appropriate level of quality, the overall level of quality should only increase. Particularly if there are vendors that can produce at a competitive price, but at higher levels of quality than GM's internal operations, outsourcing would improve the quality of the final product.

c. GM has an ethical obligation to its existing employees to be fair in its negotiations. However, if GM is not given greater flexibility to outsource, eventually its entire employee base could be in jeopardy as the inflexibility may lead to a less competitive position in the industry, especially relative to tough foreign competitors such as Toyota. Thus a loss of current jobs because of greater outsourcing may lead to more stability for the remaining jobs at GM. Furthermore, before outsourcing components, GM should evaluate whether changes in internal operations would result in sufficient improvement to diminish the need to outsource.

39. a. Quality is one of the attributes of an automobile that enters the pricing equation. It is certainly likely that a $10,000 automobile will be of lower quality than one priced at $25,000. In more developed economies, competition may focus somewhat on price, but only above some minimum threshold of quality. The presence of many world-class competitors in the developed economy ensures that some focus on quality of output is necessary. Thus, the lowest price automobile in the United States or Japan may be substantially above the price at which GM is aiming to sell the model to be produced in Brazil.

To market automobiles in both developed and underdeveloped economies, GM may pursue different strategies. While quality may be an important purchase criterion to United States consumers, price may be the predominant criterion in Third-World markets. Consequently, consumers may be unwilling and unable to bear the price of automobiles that have the same quality as those sold in the United States market.

b. The quality of GM's cars is likely to vary between developed and less developed markets. This variance simply reflects GM's responsiveness to the desires of consumers. However, GM must make certain that all cars meet minimal quality levels. GM's minimal ethical obligation is to not produce a car that is unsafe, regardless of price. Accordingly, even if the price of the automobile could be reduced by omitting basic safety features (such as seat belts), it would be unethical to sell such a car. While other dimensions of quality may be manipulated, basic safety features should not be subject to price/quality tradeoffs.

Additionally, GM must be ethical in its operations. Particularly, the firm must not exploit an absence of child labor laws or environmental protection laws to achieve its cost targets.

CHAPTER 14
RESPONSIBILITY ACCOUNTING AND TRANSFER PRICING
IN DECENTRALIZED OPERATIONS

Questions

1.   In centrally organized firms, decision making is concentrated among a few individuals--those at the top of the organizational hierarchy. In decentralized firms, the authority and responsibility for making decisions is pushed down to lower level managers. The rationale is that lower level managers have more information about their areas of the business and are in the best position to make decisions for those areas.

3.   While many skills are common to managers in centralized and decentralized firms, the decentralized manager must be willing to accept greater risk. The greater risk is associated with a performance evaluation that is based on the results achieved rather than the managerial actions taken. The managers must accept the authority to make decisions, execute the decisions, and live with the outcome. This requires the decentralized manager to be creative, goal-oriented, assertive and decisive.

5.   The costs may include the costs of poor decisions by inexperienced managers; the costs associated with a divergence between organizational, organizational segment, and individual goals (these are sometimes called agency costs or costs of suboptimization); the costs of duplicating activities across subunits; the costs of a more sophisticated planning and communication network; the costs of a more sophisticated accounting system; and the costs of training new managers.

7.   A segment manager should be evaluated only on factors (costs & revenues) that are directly traceable to his/her segment <u>and</u> under his/her control. Alternatively, the segment should be evaluated on all factors that are directly traceable to the segment <u>and</u> necessary for the segment's operation. These two sets of factors are not completely overlapping. For example, the salary of the segment manager can be traced to the segment (and is therefore used to evaluate the segment), but it is not controllable by the segment manager (and therefore is not used to evaluate the segment manager).

9.   In the broadest sense, a variance is a deviation between a planned outcome and an actual outcome. By focusing managerial attention on variances, the factors that generate a difference between the desired result and actual result can be identified. Once the causal factors are recognized, managers can take actions to exploit favorable factors and overcome unfavorable factors. Such actions should bring a closer alignment between planned and actual results.

Chapter 14
Responsibility Accounting and Transfer Pricing in Decentralized Operations

11. Suboptimization occurs when the goals of the individual manager, his/her subunit, and the organization are not in harmony. Generally, suboptimization occurs because subunit managers are too focused on maximizing the performance of their subunits rather than maximizing the performance of the overall organization. In turn, this result is often caused by imperfect incentive contracting systems (performance-based pay systems).

13. Transfer prices are internally set (agreed upon) prices with which a selling division transfers goods or services to a buying division. The role of the transfer price is to provide goal congruence while retaining subunit autonomy, and provide motivation for managers to be effective and efficient in their operations.

15. Standard costs have the advantage of being known or agreed upon in advance and of being a measure of efficient production. Actual costs may vary widely from month to month because of large changes in production volume, seasonal variations, and efficiencies.

17. Dual pricing is the permitting of the selling division to record one transfer price (higher) and the buying division to record another (lower). This practice is intended to minimize suboptimization and create goal-congruent incentives for both divisions.

19. Because transfer prices between multinational units of a company can affect profits and inventory values reported in two different countries, managers must be cognizant of setting prices, within legal and ethical limits, to minimize income taxes and tariffs.

Exercises

21. a. 4
    b. 5
    c. 10
    d. 6
    e. 7
    f. 1
    g. 3
    h. 2
    i. 9
    j. 8

Chapter 14
Responsibility Accounting and Transfer Pricing
in Decentralized Operations

23. a. D
    b. A
    c. A
    d. D
    e. D
    f. A
    g. A
    h. A
    i. A
    j. N

25. a. Price variance =
    (Expected price - Actual price) + Sales volumes
    = ($42.00 - $39.50) × 425,000
    = $1,062,500 U

    Volume variance =
    Projected price × (Projected volume - Actual volume)
    = $42 × (410,000 - 425,000)
    = $630,000 F

    b. A sales mix variance can be computed only in firms that sell more than one product; this is a single-product company.

    c. No, a determination cannot be made as to whether profits were above or below estimated levels. Information on costs would be required to make that determination.

27. a., b., c., d.

Actual sales	SP × AM × AV	SP × SM* × AV	Budgeted sales
	$40 × 30,000	$40 × 17,500	$1,800,000
	$30 × 40,000	$30 × 52,500	800,000
$2,700,000	$2,400,000	$2,275,000	$2,600,000
	$300,000 F	$125,000 F	$325,000 U
	Price variance	Mix variance	Volume variance

Total variance = $2,700,000 - $2,600,000 = $100,000 F
*SM = 25% shoes, 75% baseball gloves

29. a. The upper limit for the transfer is the lowest outside price at which the buying division can purchase a comparable water pump: $55. The lower limit is the relevant cost to produce and sell the unit: $20.40 + $4.20 + $12.60 = $37.20.

    b. $48

    c. $48 - $10.80 = $37.20

    d.   This would be a breakeven price for the Accessory Division. It would have an incentive to make the transfer only if its profits could be increased by doing so.

31.   a.   Units sold internally = $75,000 \div $1.25 = 60,000
Total production = 60,000 \div .4 = 150,000
External sales = 150,000 - 60,000 = 90,000
Internal variable costs = $30,000 \div 60,000 = $.50
External variable costs = $45,000 \div 90,000 = $.50
External sales price = $135,000 \div 90,000 = $1.50
Change in gross profit = ($1.40 - $1.25) \times 60,000
                = $9,000

    b.   ($1.25 - $1.70) \times 60,000 = $(27,000)

    c.   Transfer price = $1.25 + ($.15 \div 2)
                    = $1.325

    d.   A dual transfer price would allow the Office Supplies Division to record the internal sales at the external price of $1.40, and allow the Garden Division to record the transfer at the existing internal price, $1.25. The dual transfer pricing arrangement would provide incentive to both the buying and selling divisions to make the internal transfer.

33.   a.   A
    b.   D
    c.   A
    d.   D
    e.   A
    f.   D
    g.   A
    h.   A
    i.   D

Problems

35. a. The most significant problem is that the variances are computed by comparing the static budget to the actual expenses. To evaluate cost control, a flexible budget should be compiled at the actual level of activity. Variances should be computed by comparing the flexible budget to actual costs. An additional weakness is that the performance evaluation does not contain auxiliary performance measures including measures of product quality and customer service.

b.

	Flexible Budget	Actual	Variance
Activity level	$1,800,000	$1,800,000	$ 0
Variable Costs:			
Professional labor	$900,000	$940,000	$40,000 U
Travel	45,000	40,000	5,000 F
Supplies	90,000	90,000	0
Fixed Costs:			
Professional labor	400,000	405,000	5,000 U
Facilities cost	250,000	265,000	15,000 U
Insurance	80,000	78,000	2,000 F
Totals	$1,765,000	$1,818,000	$53,000 U

c. The variances that are most likely to be investigated are the ones that are material and may be attributed to controllable factors. The most material variances are for the variable cost of professional labor (4.44% over the flexible budget), travel (11.11% under the flexible budget), and the facilities cost (6% over budget).

d. Upper management should establish the criteria that determine which variances are to be investigated. They should be assisted in this task by managerial accountants.

37. a.

	Actual	Standard	Variance
Metal	$507,500	$420,000	$87,500 U
Galvanizing	65,800	70,000	4,200 F
Direct labor	104,300	105,000	700 F
Overhead			
Welding supplies	34,900	31,500	3,400 U
Utilities	38,300	38,500	200 F
Indirect labor	25,500	28,000	2,500 F
Machine M/R	21,200	14,000	7,200 U
Equip. depr.	77,000	77,000	0
Miscellaneous	29,500	28,000	1,500 U
	$904,000	$812,000	$92,000 U

b. Overall, Ms. Padgett generated $92,000 of costs in excess
of the budget. However, much of the excess cost may have
been beyond her control. For example, the most
significant variance is for metal. Based on the preceding
analysis, it is not possible to determine whether that
variance is due to a price or quantity factor. If the
variance for metal is largely comprised of a price
variance, it is unlikely that Ms. Padgett has control over
price. This variance should be used to evaluate the
purchasing department. This is true of all other inputs
as well. As a production supervisor, Ms. Padgett would be
responsible for the quantity of inputs used but would not
have control over the price of inputs used. Consequently,
the variance for each item should be decomposed into a
price and quantity element.

     The variances that would likely be investigated would
include metal, galvanizing, and maintenance/repair. The
key criteria to decide which variances are worthy of
investigation are controllability and magnitude. It makes
no difference if the variance is favorable or unfavorable.

39. a.

Revenues		$80,000
Variable expenses		
Meals and lodging	$36,000	
Supplies	2,000	38,000
Contribution margin		$42,000
Fixed expenses		
Speakers	$10,000	
Rent on facilities	7,200	
Advertising	4,200	21,400
Controllable segment margin		$20,600
Allocated fixed costs		5,000
Profit		$15,600

b.

Revenues		$77,000
Variable expenses		
Meals and lodging	$43,200	
Supplies	2,400	45,600
Contribution margin		$31,400
Fixed expenses		
Speakers	$15,500	
Rent on facilities	8,400	
Advertising	5,800	29,700
Controllable segment margin		$ 1,700
Allocated fixed costs		5,000
Profit		$(3,300)

c. Revenues $ 3,000 U
    Meals & Lodging   7,200 U
    Supplies   400 U
    Contribution margin $10,600 U
    Rent on facilities   1,200 U
    Advertising   1,600 U
    Speakers   5,500 U
    Controllable segment margin $18,900 U
    Allocated fixed costs   0
    Profit $18,900 U

   The factors most responsible for the difference
between budgeted and actual profit of the tax seminar are
the volume of participants and the failure to budget for
the airline costs of the speakers. The extra volume of
participants, in turn, is related to the additional
advertising and the reduction in the seminar fee.

d. It is fortunate for Professor Thomas that he is already
    tenured. Virtually all of the difference between actual
    and budgeted profit from the seminar can be attributed to
    actions taken by Professor Thomas. In addition to the
    mistake (omission of $5,000 for transporting speakers),
    Professor Thomas demonstrated a lack of knowledge of cost
    causality. By lowering the seminar fee, Professor Thomas
    pushed volume up sufficiently to cause certain fixed costs
    to rise (advertising, and rent on facilities). It doesn't
    appear that Professor Thomas was effective in managing the
    relationship between costs and activities.

41. a. ■ Current external selling price $5,400
          Selling Division--fair value since most are produced
            and sold at this price externally.
          Buying Division--price is higher than what could be
            purchased elsewhere so this would make its
            performance report appear worse than by buying
            externally.

        ■ Total variable production cost ($2,100)+ 20% = $2,520
          Selling Division--contributes minimally to covering
            fixed costs and therefore no profit is shown from
            these sales as opposed to external sales. There
            is little incentive to sell internally if the
            selling division can sell all its output
            externally.
          Buying Division--less than external purchase price;
            therefore, it is more beneficial to the bottom line
            of Heavy-Duty Equipment.

- Total product ($3,000) cost + 20% = $3,600

     Selling Division--covers some but not all costs for
     this division; therefore, incentive to sell
     internally isn't there if Motor Division can sell
     its output externally.

     Buying Division--purchase price below external, which
     is better for margin in this division.

- Bid price from external supplier ($4,800)

     Selling Division--allows for some profit which is an
     incentive to sell internally unless it can sell all
     its output externally.

     Buying Division--no incentive to buy internally
     since it costs the same to buy from an external
     supplier.

b.   Upper limit = $4,800
     Lower limit = costs of $2,400 + contribution margin of
       $3,000 = $5,400
     Since the lower limit exceeds the upper limit, the company
     would be better off not making the internal transfers.

43. a.

	Bottle	Perfume	Irresistible Scents
Revenue (6,000,000)	$ 19,980,000	$ 127,800,000	$ 127,800,000
Cost	(14,400,000)	(116,760,000)	(111,180,000)
Margin	$ 5,580,000	$ 11,040,000	$ 16,620,000
Return on sales	28%	8.6%	13%

b.   This level of operation is most profitable for the Bottle
     Division relative to sales. The Bottle Division's return
     on sales is more than three times the return on sales
     realized in the Perfume Division.

c.   The Bottle Division once existed as a separate company.
     As such it was purchased with a management control system
     intact. It may be assumed that it was left as a separate
     division for managerial control purposes--to be able to
     separately evaluate the performance of bottling from
     perfume production. However, the big question is whether
     any purpose is served in leaving the Bottle Division as a
     profit center. It would seem that many of the conflicts
     between the Bottle and Perfume Divisions could be
     eliminated if the Bottle Division were made a cost center.
     This would be appropriate since the Bottle Division has no
     outside sales; and hence, is accountable for none of the
     company's revenues.

45. a. One of the purposes of this problem is to demonstrate that the price that generates a 20% return on sales is sensitive to assumptions made about sales volume. At the existing volume (70% of capacity) fixed costs amount to $100 per unit. If this is the assumed level of operations for the coming year, the per-unit sales price that generates net income before taxes equal to 20% of sales would be:

    Let S = Sales price per unit
    S - $290 = .2S
    .8S = $290
    S = $362.50

    However, students may come up with alternative answers depending on the assumptions made with regard to volume. As volume rises, fixed costs per unit decline and the sales price required to generate a 20% return declines.

    b. As a practical matter, the highest possible price would be $260 per unit. This is the outside price and represents the cost that Conveyor Systems Division could acquire the pumps from an alternative supply source. Even though this price fails to meet the net income objectives of the Hydraulic Division, any higher price will cause the division to lose the internal business.

    c. The division should charge any price that will cause the Conveyor Systems Division to purchase internally. The company's variable cost to produce the pump is $120 + $40 + $30 = $190. Since the market price is $260, the company is $70 per unit better off if the pump is made rather than purchased. The actual transfer price is irrelevant to the determination of overall corporate profits; however, the transfer price will affect the relative profits of the buying and selling divisions. From the company perspective, any transfer price that causes the Conveyor Systems Division to purchase internally is optimal. Thus, the likely range of prices is $190 to $260.

Chapter 14
Responsibility Accounting and Transfer Pricing
in Decentralized Operations

47. a. 1. Responsibility accounting is a system of accounting that recognizes various responsibility or decision centers throughout an organization, and reflects the plans and actions of these centers by assigning particular revenues and costs to the one having the pertinent responsibility for making decisions about these revenues and costs.

2. The benefits that accrue to a company using responsibility accounting include the following:
    - The development of responsibility budgets and plans that encourage managers to plan ahead and promote goal congruence.
    - Participation in the planning process causes company guidelines to be more readily accepted as achievable.
    - The development of responsibility accounting plans that provide managers with clear guidelines for day-to-day decisions and free management from daily operations.
    - Responsibility accounting that affords management performance evaluation criteria.

3. The advantages of responsibility accounting to the managers of a firm include the following:
    - Under the guidelines of responsibility accounting, managers are responsible only for those items over which they have control.
    - Because responsibility accounting facilitates the delegation of decision making, managers are afforded greater freedom of action without daily supervision.
    - Managers know what is expected of them and on what basis their performance will be evaluated.
    - The ability to participate in decision making and to exercise control helps managers develop leadership skills.

b.   1.   The managers of Family Resorts are likely to support the budget preparation process because they are active participants in the process. The managers have been allowed to prepare and submit budgets on an autonomous basis. If major changes are needed to the budgets submitted, the managers are consulted before changes are implemented.

The features of the budget presentation that would make it attractive to the managers include the following:

- The managers are only responsible for costs that are directly under their control; arbitrary allocations have been avoided.

- The budget presentation shows the managers exactly how their segment fits into the entire company and how their units contribute to the overall well being of the firm.

- The presentation clearly depicts those areas each manager is responsible for and establishes the criteria on which his/her performance will be evaluated.

2.   Recommendations to improve the budget process might include the following:

- The budget could be presented using the contribution approach and segregating variable and fixed costs.

- There could be a comparison to prior year actuals so that managers know whether their contributions have increased or decreased.

- The expense items could be presented as a percentage of sales.

(CMA)

49. a.   Mr. Wallace believes that his obligation is to meet the overall level of budgeted cost; this means he has authority to overspend in some areas as long as there is offsetting underspending in other areas.

Mr. Driver believes that Mr. Wallace has an obligation to stay within the budget established for each item of expense. The substitution of overspending in one category for underspending in another is not permissible.

b.   The budget should be subdivided into discretionary and
nondiscretionary amounts. The nondiscretionary amounts
would be those which Mr. Wallace would have no authority to
change; the discretionary amounts would be expended subject
to the judgment of Mr. Wallace. Discretionary and
nondiscretionary amounts could be established for each
expense item or entire expense items could be classified as
discretionary or nondiscretionary. The nondiscretionary
costs would represent the activities that the management
wants conducted at a specified level. The nondiscretionary
amounts would represent those costs that could be shifted
between expense items subject to changing conditions such as
temperature, rainfall, and level of use.

c.   Depreciation is a cost that is certainly not controllable by
Mr. Wallace. This suggests that in addition to separating
budgetary amounts into discretionary and nondiscretionary
components, they should also be separated into controllable
and noncontrollable components. Mr. Wallace should not be
held accountable for noncontrollable expenses.

d.   The board of directors should be responsible for evaluating
the performance of Mr. Wallace. The board of directors
would be the committee that has responsibility for oversight
of employees and hiring and firing employees. The greens
committee's authority and responsibility should be
constrained to maintaining the physical condition of the
golf course.

51. a.   **Delaying the billing of late-year shipments** Yes, this
would delay the recognition of the revenue until 2000.

Encouraging customers to delay purchases Yes, this would
cause sales that would otherwise be made in 1999 to be
delayed until 2000.

Increasing 1999 expense accruals This would cause a shift
in income from 1999 to 2000 because the extraordinarily
large accruals in 1999 would allow the company to
recognize much smaller expense accruals in 2000.

**Purchasing raw materials that were not included in year-
ending inventory** Not including the materials in
inventory would cause 1999 income to be reduced by
overstating the actual cost of goods sold. In turn, this
will cause the 2000 cost of goods sold to be understated.
This will increase 2000 income.

Recording late-December credit sales as January sales
This will decrease revenue recognized in December and
increase revenue recognized in January. It will cause an
increase in 2000 income.

Accelerating maintenance and repairs   This increases
expenses in 1999 and decreases 2000 expenses, relative to
what they otherwise would have been.   This will cause 1999
income to decline and 2000 income to increase.

b.   The manipulations wouldn't necessarily directly hamper the
quality of operations.   However, the manipulation diverts
managerial attention from real economic issues to planning
the income shifting.   Accordingly, the manipulations allow
managers to manipulate the perception of the reality
rather than the reality itself.   The managerial talent and
energy devoted to this activity could have resulted in
improved quality of operations, decreased costs, and
greater value for customers.   Additionally, consider what
could happen to quality in subsequent years if the
managers would delay maintenance and repair activities
rather than accelerate them.

c.   These manipulations are unethical.   They are effected to
change a perception of the reality and not the reality
itself.   By changing the perception of the reality, managers
are able to obtain promotions, pay raises, and bonuses.
This is in effect stealing from stockholders because they
are obtaining the benefits of higher organizational
performance without delivering that level of performance.

53. a.   In accounting applications, there are so many alternative
definitions of the term cost, that a clarifying
explanation is mandatory.   To omit a definition of cost,
intentionally or unintentionally, can be misleading.
Accounting information should not be distorted by
definitions of terminology.

b.   Yes, Egret is clearly being unethical in the distribution
of profits.   Egret is aware of the differences in the
transfer pricing bases, and hence, he is aware that his
bonus is largely attributable to the difference in the two
transfer prices.   This is equivalent to stealing from
Swan.

c.   It is difficult to tell whether Egret's actions are
illegal.   They certainly may be illegal to the extent Swan
believes, and Egret had reinforced the idea that the
transfer prices of each are based on the same definition
of cost.

d.   The simplest recommendation would be to base the transfer price on market prices. This would allow the transfer price to be established by unbiased, impersonal market forces. This would preclude the manipulation of the price by either party. Using market price for the transfer of services would seem to be feasible given the large number of firms that provide these types of services; market prices should be readily available. Additionally, the use of market price would allow Egret and Swan to make better decisions regarding insourcing or outsourcing services. The use of market price should reduce Egret's bonus and increase Swan's bonus.

55. Allocation of computer service costs should be made on some kind of an hours-used basis to permit a more efficient use of company resources. The changing basis should encourage users to take advantage of the Computer Systems Department's services but not permit the Computer Systems Department to pass on its inefficiencies. For instance, a standard hourly usage rate should be developed on past experience, adjusted for efficiency considerations. Divisions would be charged the standard rate for the hours of recorded usage.

(CMA adapted)

CHAPTER 15
MEASURING AND REWARDING PERFORMANCE

Questions

1. The measurement system should
   - assess progress toward achievement of organizational goals and objectives;
   - be based on the input of those being evaluated;
   - consider the skills, information and authority of those being evaluated; and
   - provide necessary feedback in a timely and useful manner to managers.

3. Because managerial pay is linked to their performance, managers will take actions to maximize their *measured* performance. This is why selection of performance measures is so important; if the wrong measures are selected, managers will attempt to maximize less important dimensions of performance. The selected measures should be the ones that are most highly correlated with the organization's goals and objectives.

5. Manipulation is an important concern because performance measures should be designed to capture only real performance, not manipulation of the performance measure. If a performance measure can be manipulated by managers, then they can achieve a high level of measured performance by either performing very well or by manipulating the measure. External measures are far superior to interior measures in this respect; they are not susceptible to internal manipulation.

7. The major difference between a profit and an investment center is that the investment center has control over costs, revenues and the level of assets employed. Accordingly, investment centers need to be evaluated based on their profitability relative to the value of assets used. Profit centers have no responsibility for assets and can be evaluated based on profit alone.

9. The DuPont model is a formulation of the return on investment (ROI) ratio. In the DuPont model, ROI is the product of profit margin multiplied by asset turnover. Each component ratio provides information on a distinct dimension of performance. The profit margin measures how much of each sales dollar was turned into profit; the asset turnover ratio is a measure of asset utilization and captures how many dollars of asset investment were required to generate each dollar of sales.

11. Suboptimization may be created in using ROI because the
     divisional ROIs differ from the overall organization's ROI.
     In such a circumstance, a division may invest (fail to invest)
     in new assets when, from the perspective of the overall
     organization's ROI, it would have been better not to invest
     (to invest). ROI is most likely to create a suboptimization
     problem in firms where the target and achieved levels of ROI
     vary substantially from one division to another. This problem
     is likely to be minimized when there is little variance among
     all the divisions' ROIs.

13. Some of the performance measures the company might adopt
     include the following: first-pass rejection rate, number of
     customer returns, number of units scrapped or rejected, number
     of units reworked, and input waste and shrinkage.

15. The only way quality can be built into a product is to have a
     high quality design and high quality conversion processes.
     Costs incurred to achieve a high quality design and processes
     are quality prevention costs. Because quality cannot be
     inspected into or out of products, prevention expenditures are
     the only value-adding quality costs. Failure costs represent
     absence of quality and inspection costs represent uncertainty
     about quality.

17. Multinational companies have substantially more issues to deal
     with than companies operating only in one country. Among the
     important factors that may vary from country to country are:
     culture, religion, labor laws, tax laws, work ethic,
     individual freedoms, market stability, political stability,
     inflation and exchange rates, financing costs, and consumer
     wealth. In designing performance evaluation measures, both
     the organizational goals, and the local conditions and
     constraints need to be considered. Thus, performance measures
     will need to be tailored to fit the local circumstances.

19. By owning stock in the corporation, managers have incentive to
     think like stockholders. Providing stock to managers is a
     widely used method to maintain compatibility between the
     incentives and motivations of managers and owners.

Exercises

21. a. 10
     b.   5
     c.   4
     d.   6
     e.   9
     f.   1
     g.   3
     h.   2
     i.   7
     j.   8

23.   a.   ($14,400,000 - $13,004,000) ÷ $14,400,000 = <u>9.70%</u>

     b. $14,400,000 ÷ $3,600,000 = <u>4</u>

     c.   9.70% × 4 = <u>38.8%</u>

25.   a.   Segment Margin = Average Assets × ROI
          Segment Margin = $3,400,000 × .125 = <u>$425,000</u>

     b.   Total Revenues = Segment Margin + Direct Expenses
          Total Revenues = $425,000 + $1,275,000 = <u>$1,700,000</u>

     c.   Asset Turnover = Total Revenues ÷ Average Assets
          Asset Turnover = $1,700,000 ÷ $3,400,000 = <u>.50</u>

     d.   Profit Margin = Segment Margin ÷ Total Revenues
          Profit Margin = $425,000 ÷ $1,700,000 = <u>25%</u>

     e.   ROI = Asset Turnover × Profit Margin
          ROI = .50 × 25% = <u>12.5%</u>

27.   a.   North Division: $30,000 - ($180,000 × .12) = <u>$ 8,400</u>
          South Division: $68,000 - ($290,000 × .12) = <u>$33,200</u>

     b.   Based on the residual income criterion, the South
          Division is more successful.

29.   EVA = After-tax Income - (Target Return × Invested Capital)
     EVA = $1,800,000 - (.16 × $12,000,000)
     EVA = $1,800,000 - $1,920,000 = <u>$(120,000)</u>

31. a.   **EVA by Year:**
        Year 1: $800,000 - ($8,000,000 × .13)   = $(240,000)
        Year 2: $800,000 - ($8,000,000 × .13)   = $(240,000)
        Year 3: $1,160,000 - ($8,000,000 × .13) = $ 120,000
        Year 4: $2,900,000 - ($8,000,000 × .13) = $1,860,000
        Year 5: $2,700,000 - ($8,000,000 × .13) = $1,660,000

     b.   **Compensation by Year:**
        Year 1: $(240,000)   × .12 = $(28,800)
        Year 2: $(240,000)   × .12 = $(28,800)
        Year 3: $ 120,000   × .12 = $14,400
        Year 4: $1,860,000 × .12 = $223,200
        Year 5: $1,660,000 × .12 = $199,200

    c.   Whether Ms. Jenks will be hesitant to invest or not depends largely on her personal time horizon. Although investing in the project would reduce her compensation during the first three years, this reduction would be more than offset in the last two years. If Ms. Jenks' time horizon is three years or less, she is unlikely to invest. If her time horizon is four years or more, she is likely to invest. Also, Ms. Jenks must deal with the possibility that she would be dismissed from her position in one of the first three years due to poor performance if she invests in the project.

    d.   Yes. Upper management would likely view the project favorably. The project appears to generate a return far in excess of the cost of capital after Year 2.

    e.   Some measures that could be adopted include growth in market share, growth in sales, number of new customers served, rate of customer retention, and customer satisfaction rates.

33.   **Performance**   **Explanation**

    a.   Q   This measure captures the quality of production processes.

    b.   CS   Percent on-time shipments measures how frequently customers are receiving their goods when they were promised receipt.

    c.   RM   Manufacturing cycle time captures the extent to which a firm is using its available capacity.

    d.   Q   This measure captures the percentage of units started that are completed and nondefective.

    e.   Q   This is a measure of process quality.

    f.   RM   Output per labor dollar measures the efficiency of utilizing direct labor.

    g.   Q or CS   Number of crisis calls measures the rate of product failure.

    h.   F   Changeover time measures how flexible production systems are in changing from the production of one product to another.

    i.   RM   Machine downtime represents wasted productive capacity.

    j.   Q   Supplier rejects measures the quality of product design and production processes for incoming components and materials.

35.   a.   Has no effect on turnover.

    b.   Decreases the turnover ratio relative to what it could be if the unused assets were sold.

    c.   Decreases the turnover ratio relative to what it would be if the obsolete inventory were sold.

    d.   Decreases the turnover ratio.

    e.   Increases the turnover ratio.

    f.   Has no effect on the turnover ratio.

37. No answer provided. The purpose of the exercise is to cause the student to contemplate how he/she would deliver feedback to a subordinate.

Problems

39. a. asset turnover =
    $$\$13,440,000 \div [(\$9,600,000 + \$12,800,000) \div 2] = \underline{1.2}$$

    profit margin = ($13,440,000 - $12,499,200) ÷ $13,440,000
    $$= \underline{7.0\%}$$

    ROI = 1.2 × 7% = <u>8.4%</u>

    The Material Handling Division failed to achieve the industry norm for either the profit margin or the asset turnover.

    b. The most likely area to improve performance is in asset utilization. It should be noted, however, that the asset level increased substantially during the year and asset utilization for 1999 may be underestimated by the asset turnover ratio (particularly if a substantial portion of the increase in assets occurred near the end of the year). The division must also try to improve profitability. Its profit as a percentage of sales was a full point below the norm for the industry. Improved profitability may result from either greater volume or reduced costs.

41. a. Average assets =
    ($3,600,000 + $4,400,000) ÷ 2 = $4,000,000

    ROI = $800,000 ÷ $4,000,000 = <u>20%</u>

    b. ROI = ($400,000 - $200,000 - $100,000) ÷ $620,000
    = <u>16.13%</u> (rounded)

    c. ROI = ($800,000 + $100,000) ÷ ($4,000,000 + $620,000)
    = <u>19.48%</u> (rounded)

    d. The Odessa Divisional manager will not want to add the new line. In doing so, the division manager's bonus would be reduced because the new asset would lower the division's overall ROI.

    The President would like to see the new product line added. This is because the new asset would generate an ROI of 16.13% which is greater than the corporate-wide existing ROI of 15%. Consequently, the overall corporate ROI would rise with the new asset in place.

    To summarize, each manager sees the new asset as desirable or undesirable based on its expected effect on his/her ROI. While the new asset would raise the corporate ROI, and an evaluation measure of the corporate president, it would lower the division's ROI, and the evaluation measure of the divisional manager.

Chapter 15
Measuring and Rewarding Performance

43. a. $1.5 \times 8\% = \underline{12\%}$

    b. Asset Turnover = Sales ÷ Average Assets
       = $\$6,000,000 \div [(\$2,400,000 + \$3,600,000) \div 2]$
       = $\$6,000,000 \div \$3,000,000$
       = $\underline{2}$
       Profit Margin = Segment Margin ÷ Sales
       = $(\$6,000,000 - \$5,640,000) \div \$6,000,000$
       = $\underline{6\%}$
       ROI = $2 \times 6\% = \underline{12\%}$

       The actual ROI was in line with the expected level;
       however, the asset turnover exceeded the target level
       while the profit margin was below the target level.

    c. The profit margin was the area where performance was
       below expectations. The division needs to work to
       improve its operational efficiency either by cutting
       costs or increasing volume.

    d.
Segment margin	$360,000
less target return ($3,000,000 × .13)	(390,000)
Residual income	$(30,000)

45. a. Pleasure ROI = $(\$12,000,000 - \$10,800,000) \div \$10,000,000$
                     = $\underline{12\%}$
       Commercial ROI = $(\$48,000,000 - \$42,000,000) \div \$30,000,000$
                      = $\underline{20\%}$

    b. The manager of Pleasure Division is the most likely to
       invest in a new project. Such an investment would
       increase the overall ROI of the division. The manager of
       Commercial Division would not invest because the
       projected ROI on the new project is lower than the
       projected divisional ROI.

    c. Such an outcome is inconsistent with overall corporate
       goals. Company-wide, the projected ROI is: ($60,000,000
       - $52,800,000) ÷ $40,000,000 = 18%. Thus the company
       would probably want the manager of Commercial Division to
       make the investment and would prefer that the manager of
       Pleasure Division reject the investment.

d.   If the division managers were evaluated on the basis of
      residual income, they would analyze how a new investment
      would affect the projected overall RI level in their
      divisions.   The projected overall changes could be found
      as follows:

	Pleasure	Commercial
Projected ROI on new project	14%	18%
Required target return	17%	17%
Residual return	-3%	1%

Thus, according to the projections, the project under
evaluation by the manager of Pleasure Division would
cause his/her overall residual income to decline by an
amount equal to 3 percent of the cost of the investment.
On the other hand, the project under consideration by the
manager of Commercial Division would generate an overall
increase in RI equal to 1 percent of the cost of the new
investment.

47.   a.   Manufacturing cycle efficiency
                  = Processing time ÷ Total time
                  = 80,000 ÷ 120,000
                  = 67% (rounded)

      b.   Process productivity = Total units ÷ Processing time
                              = 200,000 ÷ 80,000
                              = 2.5

      c.   Process quality yield = Good units ÷ Total units
                               = 130,000 ÷ 200,000
                               = 65%

      d.   2.5 × .67 × .65 = 1.09 units per hour (rounded)

      e.   The existence of a bottleneck would most likely be
            reflected in Part b, process productivity.

      f.   Defective units would be reflected in the ratio of good
            units to total units, Process quality yield - Part c.

Chapter 15
Measuring and Rewarding Performance

Cases

49. a.   For 1999, NOC generated an ROI of 25 percent, as calculated below:

ROI = Operating income ÷ Total assets

    = \$2,000,000 ÷ \$8,000,000

    = <u>25%</u>

For 1999, assuming NOC paid \$3.2 million for RLI, it would have generated an ROI of less than 20 percent, as calculated below:

ROI = Operating income ÷ Total assets

    = \$600,000 ÷ \$3,200,000

    = <u>18.75%</u>

Mr. Grieco would have expected that his bonus would be lost or reduced if he had invested in RLI. The investment would have caused the ROI of NOC to drop as indicated below:

Combined ROI = Operating income ÷ Total assets

             = \$2,600,000 ÷ \$11,200,000

             = <u>23.21%</u>

  b.   To determine the effect of the acquisition, one only needs to determine the amount of residual income generated by RLI:

Operating income	\$600,000
Target return (\$3,200,000 × .15)	<u>(480,000)</u>
Residual income generated by RLI	<u>\$120,000</u>

Because the Residual Income is positive, the acquisition of RLI would have had a positive effect on Mr. Grieco's bonus expectations.

  c.   No, it is the duty of top management to provide incentives to Mr. Grieco such that if it is in the best interest of Allston Automotive to invest, it is also in the best interest of Mr. Grieco to invest. Such is not the case with the ROI performance measure.

  d.   No, the present system heavily biases against new investment in anything. The best way managers can protect their current ROI levels is to not invest.

(CMA)